Introduction and

This book has been taken me a decade to write. Thanks to Alfred Thompson who inspired me to finally get it off the ground.

Disclaimer: *I am a Computer Science teacher, not an English teacher,* which means that I wrote this book like I *wanted to write it.* I probably violated numerous protocols, writing styles, and book publishing norms. I loooooove my punctuation marks, especially -- ... ; ! and (.) You might also find a few hidden misspellings, unintended oops, or grammatically "odd" sentences. My writing sounds a lot like I do when I talk, so that part is on purpose! I wanted my passion for Computer Science to come through to give *whoever reads this* the encouragement to just *GO FOR IT*!

If something I say in the book resonates with you, you have questions, want to see some pictures or video examples of ideas in the book, want to discuss pedagogy or ideology, or simply want to connect, please find me at www.innovativeteacher.org

Testimonials

Lou Zulli • Technology Director • IT Instructor and Network Administrator for the Center of Advanced Technologies at Lakewood High School St. Petersburg, FL. (Retired)

"There are teachers or educators and then there is Doug Bergman. This book reflects his infectious enthusiasm, his boundless energy and the depth of his expertise, which is built on years of experience with spectacular results. In these pages, Doug shares his award winning technique, his philosophy and his instructional design."

Lindsay Bayne • Microsoft Education

"Preparing students for future digital careers and showing how Computer Science is necessary for preparing all our future leaders is more important than ever before. Doug not only provides the resources to start preparing students in CS, but also shares why empowering them to pursue careers in computer science is important and can be done by anyone in an approachable and real way.

Mary Beth Westmoreland • Chief Technology Officer, Blackbaud

"This book is a testament to Doug's authentic passion for making Computer Science accessible to everyone. He provides useful references, relatable stories and a wealth of personal experience to help teachers deliver an engaging, inclusive and effective CS curriculum. Whether you're new to the field, or you're an experienced CS teacher, you're sure to find pragmatic, unique advice to inspire and motivate your students. We need more teachers like Doug!

Christopher Starr, PhD • Associate Professor of Information Management, Associate Chair • Supply Chain and Information Management • Director, Interdisciplinary Center for Applied Technology, School of Business, College of Charleston, S.C.

"Finally! The one book that integrates the nature of computer science with academic and experiential learning outcomes, pedagogical innovation, and tactical implementation guidelines for K12 teachers, department chairs,

principles/headmasters, district administrators and school boards. A must read for professional development for K12 teachers and administrators who seek to improve the impact of K12 education and the future of their students."

Elizabeth Hill • CS student at Clemson University, S.C.

"As a former student who has gone through 4 years of Bergman's CS courses, I can genuinely say that his passions for teaching CS to young and inquisitive minds is so outstanding, and apparent in this book. I've seen firsthand that the methods in which he presents the information to his students is able to light the tech spark we never knew we had. Before his courses, I had no idea how much untapped potential and passion I had for CS, and now I am one of only a handful of women about to graduate from college with a degree in Computer Science. I owe it all to him for showing me this amazing field! "

Pat Yongpradit • Chief Academic Officer, Code.org

"Teachers new to Computer Science can take heart that Doug has provided a down-to-earth guide for thriving in the world of computer science education that builds off his rich, personal experience."

Adam Michlin • Computer Science Teacher • Golda Och Academy • West Orange, NJ • President, Central CSTA NJ

"Doug has written a book that all experienced CS teachers wish we had years ago to help us plot or paths but especially to educate other teachers and administrators as to the unique nature of what we do and what we require. Whether you are brand new to Computer Science education or experienced, his book offers wonderful advice for anyone looking to add Computer Science to their curriculum or to enhance Computer Science offerings already in their curriculum."

James T. McKim • Operations/Strategy/PMO Lead, Hewlett Packard Enterprise Technical Learning Services

"Whether you are a teacher, school administrator, or student of education, this book will help you understand the impact Computer Science has had on our society and how you can help students get involved in doing Computer Science to make the world a better place. Doug draws on his experience *implementing successful Computer Science programs to make a convincing case regarding the need for Computer Science education in grades K-12. He provides a comprehensive plethora of practical tips for the implementation of Computer Science programs that teach the skills organizations look for in assembling a competitive workforce."*

Aaron Maurer • STEM Lead Mississippi AEA

"In a market that overwhelms the educator looking to get started in computer science, Doug has crafted a book that speaks to all backgrounds to help make the first step into computer science exciting. This book reads like a conversation with the author where you walk feeling excited about the possibilities that computer science can provided for students of all ages."

Kari Stubbs, PhD • Vice President, Learning and Innovation • BrainPOP

"It's an honor to recommend Doug' work, as I've had the pleasure of walking alongside his students as they've embraced the potential, passion, and "rolling up their sleeves" type of CS learning that we'd all dream of for our kids. I encourage you to absorb and apply his ideas, as you take the conceptual understanding of CS to a more practical reality."

Julie Hembree • M.Ed. Teacher-Librarian, Microsoft Innovative Expert • Skype & Surface Expert Educator • Cougar Ridge Elementary School, Washington

*"Educators if you are ready to rock the Computer Science world for your students, then **Imagining Computer Science Education K-12** is a must read. Doug outlines what a school needs to bring CS to the forefront of academics, the qualifications and hiring process plus professional development opportunities available throughout the country. This is a book that will intentionally ignite your passion for CS with detailed ideas on how to implement a program for your students. If you are ready to take the leap, then this book is a MUST read!"*

Jeff Tozzi • Vice President Microsoft Corporation

'While the world around us continues to go through an amazing digital transformation, unfortunately the curriculum and structure of our education system has been slow to keep pace with the skills our students need both

now as well as in the future. Doug's book outlines the critical thinking that teachers, administrators and parents alike must understand for us to have a real path forward. As Doug passionately makes the case, we must embrace the potential for what Computer Science can bring to a competitive educational system.'

Jake Baskin • Executive Director CSTA

"This is a great guide to setting up a project-based CS program in your school. Doug's experiences capture the pitfalls to avoid and best practices every teacher, school and district should be considering as they implement computer science programs."

Andi Li • Curriculum Leader, Po Leung Kuk Dr.Jimmy Wong Chi-Ho Primary School, Hong Kong

"This book is the easy way to get you into the CS world! Read it!"

Alfred Thompson • CS Teacher, Bishop Guertin High School, NJ

"Doug has created one of the most innovative and successful high school computer science curriculums around. In this book, Doug provides information for creating or improving computer science programs based on school proven ideas. The book provides insights not just from Doug's experience but also from a number of other top educators teaching in a variety of environments. This book is a must read for school boards, administrators, educators, and anyone else who wants to create a top notch computer science program that prepares students for the future."

Sebastian van Delden, PhD • CS *Department Chair and Professor, College of Charleston, S.C.*

"Doug has put together an easy-to-read resource that will enable any teacher to launch or improve a K12 computer science curriculum. In addition to providing a detailed case-study of an exemplar program, this one-stop reference manual pulls together broad surveys of contemporary technologies and support resources. Well done!"

Andrew Ko • Managing Director Global Education - WW Public Sector at Amazon Web Services

"Doug is an incredible educator with a tremendous passion for teaching and learning through the practices of computer science. This book exemplifies his knowledge and energy for the subject and will make you want to learn how to code right away"

Mike Zamansky • Coordinator of Computer Science Teacher Education, Hunter College • Architect of the computer science program at NYC's Stuyvesant High School

K12 education is experiencing two revolutions. One is the introduction of Computer Science and the other is project based learning. Doug Bergman, one of the most experienced and respected K12 CS educators is Mr. Experiential Learning. This book will guide educators of all levels into the world of both computer science education and project based or experiential learning. Doug provides road maps to go from neophyte to master in the classroom and in the greater education community. Specific in class lesson examples are also provided to jump start teachers towards become masters at creating immersive educational experiences. We needed this book decades ago!!!!

Contents

Whom is this book for?

There are two types of people who will benefit from this book:

NYC: (**N**ot **Y**et **C**onvinced)

> This educator does not really understand (or misunderstands) what Computer Science (CS) is or how CS relates to the world. This educator is still exploring if, how, and why it fits into the academics in his/her school. In the first section of the book, I'll define and describe CS, try to persuade you of its importance in our schools, as well as discuss numerous real world examples. I'll also show you what CS can look like when done right in a school.

RTR and **RTC**: (**R**eady **t**o **R**ock and **R**eady **t**o **C**hange)

> This educator understands the value of Computer Science in the bigger picture, but needs guidance in the actual design and implementation of a CS class or program. This educator might already have experience teaching Computer Science, but is looking for new, fresh, innovative, and creative approaches for his/her classroom. In this section, I'll discuss how to approach:

- Figuring out what type of CS program makes sense at your school
- Understanding options for curriculum, both off-the-shelf and creating your own.
- Understanding options for pedagogical style of your classroom
- Looking at some of the engaging technologies you can explore for use in your classroom
- Planning next steps for actually designing and implementing an innovative, project-based Computer Science program.
- Increasing enrollment, reaching new types of students

The goals of the book

Define and describe what Computer Science is
Describe what it looks like in the real world
Describe what it can look like in the classroom.
Describe what project-based CS looks like.

I'll help you research, define, design, and implement your own project-based Computer Science program. Central to that is identifying appropriate curriculum options and pedagogical style. This includes exploring the benefits of building your own curriculum, as well as using well-established off-the-shelf curriculum. There are so many excellent options; I'll help you sift through some of those. Throughout the book, you'll find plenty of resources to help you identify and compare technologies that make sense to use in your school, regardless of your budget. I'll also take a look at professional development and training available to get teachers ready for their new Computer Science classes. You'll hear from several teachers who have been down this path and can talk about what they have done. I'll share in detail how my school has implemented a project-based Computer Science program in grades 1-12. We'll even take a deep dive into several case studies of several of my specific projects, so you can see what this looks like day to day.

What is incredibly exciting about Computer Science is that it is a discipline that is constantly changing. Even as I wrote this book, new technologies came onto the market. Some of these specific technologies, languages, or sites may be out of date or even offline within a year or two, but the pedagogical style and fundamental design ideas will continue to make sense regardless of technology.

Section One

What is Computer Science?

I am using the term Computer Science (CS) in this book to represent all the major areas related to Computer Science. At the college level, there are specific areas that students can focus on. In K-12 education (and in this book) all of these areas help define the space we are referring to in this book as "Computer Science." For purposes of this book, I am referring to any class that brings together technology, ideas, hardware, software, coding, problems, and people. As you will see, it is an open-ended, flexible, and inclusive definition. Here is a partial list of these majors:

Computer Information Systems	Information Technology
Computer Science	Information Science
Management Information Systems	Big Data
Computing Systems	Medical/Health Informatics
Computing in the Arts	Game Design
Bioinformatics	Computational Science
Data Science	Programming
Computer Engineering	Networking
Software Engineering	Algorithms
Web Design	3D Printing and Design
Cybersecurity	Maker Space
	Cloud Computing

One of the not-so-obvious issues related to Computer Science is that many people confuse "technology," "Computer Science," and "digital literacy." The confusion stems just from those folks not understanding what CS is. Tools such as word processing, presentations, spreadsheets, and movie editing are excellent tools to be used in other disciplines, but they are **not** Computer Science. The best place to learn how to use these applications is in the subject areas that use them most. For example, word processing, keyboarding, and desktop publishing should be taught in the English classroom. Presentation software should be taught in a class where presentations and idea communication are common, such as public speaking, history, language, or English. What better place to use spreadsheets than in the math classroom, perhaps even in place of the calculator? Art class is an excellent place to learn digital image creation, graphic design, and photo manipulation. Rehearsing oral components of foreign language is an excellent use of video and audio file creation and editing. Certainly there are turf issues and time considerations having one discipline teach others' content, but don't we already do this? History and English classes both teach students how to write essays, right? Chemistry and Physics use some serious math, so they have to teach those math skills. Until the average person starts to understand the difference between Computer Science and technology and digital literacy, we need to make conscious efforts to move *applications* out of the CS classroom.

So, what then *is* Computer Science?

Technology itself changes so rapidly that what we actually study and *how* we study that content continues to evolve as well. This is important because our experience in other disciplines tends to be very different. In math, there is a clearly known and defined sequence: pre-algebra, algebra, geometry, trigonometry, and calculus. Under "science," are biology, chemistry, geology, and physics. Under "language" are grammar, literature, writing, and poetry, and vocabulary. The majority of that content is static and unchanging. It is not necessarily a *good or bad* thing, it's just a *thing*. In the English classroom, the writings of Shakespeare and Poe have been studied for decades and will continued to be studied for decades to come. The CS classroom is dramatically different; it is ever-changing and evolving.

Bringing together creativity, problem solving, software, hardware, and ideas under the same umbrella---that is **Computer Science**. The problems can be small and simple, or they can large and life changing. So it's more of a description rather than a definition. No matter the technology, there are ways of both using the technology, and there are ways of diving deeper and actually creating something with that technology. Computer Science is a set of tools and a way of thinking that gives people the ability to (re)program and command technology to identify and address problems and issues in the world around them. It is a way for an average person to accomplish above average challenges. *Computer Scientists know how to take ideas in their mind and bring them to life on a device in front of them; they can build their own tools.*

There was a time when the only people who had any chance of getting anywhere with computers were the research scientists who might spend endless days programming, tinkering, and then waiting patiently for some type of confusing output. That complexity and inaccessibility is where many of our stereotypes come from. For decades, it was like that. It was just not attractive for the average person. For those who were interested in technology and using it to solve problems, there was such a high "entrance cost" (time, money, access, frustration, resources), that they did not go into that field. Consequently, we did not get much diversity of people (or ideas) and we saw technology develop in a certain one-sided way. Had there been more diversity (gender, age, culture, religion, race, interests), who knows what our technology might look like now? With a wider variety of people starting to enter this field, I feel like we are on the verge of a new and different technological revolution.

Students in our schools right now should be the ones driving that revolution!

As technology has found its way into mainstream society, different people have taken an interest. The barriers to entering the field are coming down and the technology itself is finally becoming more accessible, more user friendly, and more "developer" friendly. In other words, it does not take a PhD in to work with it.

...and that is why you are reading this book.

Technology is in our daily conversations, movies, jokes, books, newspapers, TV shows, and especially in our schools. Schools don't need to be fearful of, restrict, or limit this technology. Quite the opposite; teach people in our schools how to use it better and differently; teach people how to address the problems of the world through that technology.

The true hard-core Computer Science person, even today, is still that person who loves his/her technology more than most, who is willing to dive deeper than most, who will stick with figuring things out longer than most. They are the people who will help us push the envelope to make new breakthroughs. This person will always have a place in industry. This person is an EXPERT at the deepest level in Computer Science. As we always have, we need lots of those people, but we also need lots of *another type* of person.

------ this is where you and your school play a part ------

The demand is huge for students who have blended their understanding and love for Computer Science with another area, such as biology, history, real estate, exercise, math, language, nature, business, chemistry, art, or any other topic. This is the person who "gets" technology, is very familiar with programming languages, has experience creating things using technology, is comfortable opening up a device and looking inside, and can put these together to address and solve the problems of any industry. This is the person who is going to introduce new products in the health and fitness market because of their command of Computer Science. This is the person who is going to develop new types of exhibitions in museums because of their command of Computer Science. This is the person who is going to revolutionize the real estate sales market with new types of selling and presentation tools because of their command of Computer Science. This is the person who is going to figure out the next breakthrough in realism in video and open up new markets in the entertainment industry because of their command of Computer Science. This is the person who is going to revolutionize the grocery store checkout with new ways for people to use technology to fill their refrigerators.

The demand for students with Computer Science experience and skills far outpaces supply, and it is only going to increase. To address this shortage, we have to bring Computer Science into schools. Not just in high school, but in middle school, and even elementary school. Not just in an occasional school, all schools. And not just for a few students, for many. Writing a program should be as common as writing an essay.

Start early. Start early. Start early.

But...please just START!

Let's take a quick peek at what CS, coding, and programming really is. I'll dive deeper later in the book, but here is one excellent resource you will use frequently in your classes.

> CODE.ORG promotes an *Hour of Code* initiative in which millions of people try their first coding experience using easy to follow beginner tutorials led by famous people from every industry. It is intended as a "hook" for first-time inexperienced students, so as an adult you should be fine to explore this: https://code.org/learn. *Right now, why not put the book down* and spend a few minutes trying to code a Star Wars or Frozen game, creating an app, or programming a virtual robot?

Ok, you're back! Did you enjoy seeing some famous people lead you through your coding exercises? That Hour of Code (or any introductory CS class) might give you a brief simple exposure to some high level CS. That is important just to lure people into diving deeper, perhaps taking a class, researching online, or learning a new technological skill. It is very important for you to see the other end of this so we can understand the bigger picture value of CS in the real world.

Computer Science in the real world

Computer Science is part of the backbone of almost every industry on the planet. I can't think of any industry that is not tremendously dependent on technology. Someone has to brainstorm, design, create, implement, demonstrate, market, sell, support, and advertise those products. So regardless of the passions and interests of students, Computer Science can give students an incredibly valuable set of tools to help them contribute in their chosen fields.

Here are some examples of Computer Science in the real world:

Farming:
Robots, through a combination of camera, image processing and sensors are able to scan an area of farming soil, detect the exact nutrition, determine the exact point in development of a seedling, determine how much light is needed, and even add extra nutrients. They are so precise that multiple crops can be planted within inches of each other. This technology allows farming to happen in ways not possible before. So students who are drawn to the world of agriculture can use their understanding of Computer Science to help plants grow better.

Public Safety:
Drones can be programmed to navigate a burning building to bring water at heights and levels of precision never before possible. They can deliver medical supplies to victims of natural disaster. They can deliver food and water to inaccessible areas. In Australia, a drone delivered a life preserver to a drowning boy. They can provide laser precision instruments guided by long distance doctors for battlefield surgery. So students who are drawn to the world of public safety can use their understanding of Computer Science to solve problems.

Crime Scene Investigation:

VR(Virtual reality) software allows police to map a crime scene, place virtual markers , and even scan evidence. This software allows evidence contamination to be reduced, as well as allows a detective to "revisit" and actually wander around the virtual crime scene in real 3D. So students who are drawn to the world of public service and safety can use their Computer Science to help people.

Real Estate:
Potential buyers can visit any house in MLS and take a virtual tour from the comfort of their own home. Architects can design structures to be viewed through VR goggles as if you were actually walking through the construction. Software can congregate current real estate data through (A) rtifical (I) ntelligence and provide answers to questions that otherwise would not be possible to know. So students who are drawn to the world of real estate and development can use their understanding of Computer Science to bring real estate properties to life in creative ways.

Retail:
A clothing or jewelry store can project a garment onto a live video feed so a person can see exactly what they would look like wearing an article of clothing or piece of jewelry without having to go through the process of actually putting it on. Grocery stores can interact with smart appliances such as the refrigerator to determine when certain products are needed and have them delivered automatically, all based on customer preference. So students who are attracted to the retail world can use their understanding of Computer Science to help companies redefine engagement with their customers

Restaurants:
One of the top complaints by customers in the foodservice industry is the speed and accuracy of the bill and checkout. Smart tablets can allow customers to order and pay with no time delay and 100% accuracy. OpenSeat allow patrons to reserve their own seats before arriving. Another food service app recommends a wine based on their selected dinner choice. You can take a picture of a meal and the

software will determine the recipe of ingredients. So students who are drawn to the world of hospitality can use their understanding of Computer Science to enhance the experience of eating.

Helping people with disabilities:
Amputees and paralyzed persons can control prosthetic limbs through their own muscle or artificial impulses generated by thought processes. Apps for people with autism help them through daily life in ways such as recommending conversational responses, guiding for sequences in executive function, recognizing facial expressions, or detecting emotions. So students who want to help people with emotional, learning, mental and physically challenges can use their understanding of Computer Science to make lives better.

Entertainment
Computer Generated Imagery creates visual effects and graphics so real they cannot be distinguished by the human eye, allowing producers to include elements in movies that could otherwise not be possible. The music industry uses software to record and edit songs. Apps like Shazam and Siri can tell you with almost 100% accuracy the name of any song after just a couple seconds. In fact, there is A.I. that actually analyzed thousands of classical music scores and used that understanding to write a computer generated musical score. Some of the world's greatest pieces of art were scanned and analyzed to determine characteristics of great art. The computer was actually able to create its own piece of art based on those results. Sites such as Spotify can interpret patterns of listeners in order to make listening recommendation. So students who are drawn to the world of entertainment can use their understanding of Computer Science to bring the arts into our lives in new ways.

Philanthropy:
Software is used to design systems for managing soup kitchens, food closets, and homeless shelter beds. Cities can more efficiently serve their poverty stricken and down-on-their-luck citizens. So students

who are drawn to the nonprofit world can use their understanding of Computer Science to solve problems that every city faces.

Politics:

Government official negotiating internationally can capture emotion, intonation, and emphasis through real-time live translation in ways that human interpretation simply cannot do. Online voting systems have to provide access while also providing security so results are valid. The new field of Big Data gives us new tools to be able to detect patterns, trends, and understanding of the mass amounts of information generated every minute. Computer Science helps identify coming weather emergencies, disease outbreaks, economic trends, and population feedback. Leaders can use this information to make decisions and help citizens feel safe and informed. Cybersecurity experts have been studying the "Russian" connection throughout the Trump administration. Those systems have to block and detect inconsistencies so infiltration can be identified before damage can be done. Facebook turned over to the FBI advertising data related to the election campaign. Algorithms used to display ads suddenly are front page news. The understanding of how Computer Science is part of this is crucial to being able to interpret intent, capability, and interference. Computer Science can help recognize trends and make predictions. So students who are drawn to the world of politics and governance can use their understanding of Computer Science to allow the people to have confidence in their governments.

Academics:

Universities and colleges across the world have made some of their most popular courses available to the public via the world wide web. Suddenly the *digital divide*, which leads to *knowledge divide*, can help bring life-changing education to populations that might not have access to education. Speakers from industry, experts in technology, and leaders of companies can virtually Skype into a classroom for live Q&A, thus bringing the real world into the classroom like never before. Students can virtually perform lab experiments that would not be possible in real life. For example, we can mix chemicals together that would normally produce toxic results. We can cut into animal organ to see inside. We can open up a car engine while it is running to see how it works. We can relive a live Roman gladiator fight. We can watch a pre-recorded speech by Martin Luther King as if we were sitting in the front row. We can explore the relationships between formulas and variables in math by using our own body to manipulate values to see the effects while immersed in a 3D virtual reality "living" chart. We can take apart a human skull or animal skeleton to see how it is constructed. Students of music can use special software to analyze their musical practice to ensure that they are playing the correct notes at the correct pitch and frequency. This software allows them to practice at home and still have "teacher" guidance. So students who are attracted to the world of education can use their understanding of Computer Science to engage teachers and students.

Sports & fitness:
People wear bracelets that can analyze their movement, health, and behavior throughout the day. Elite athletes can analyze their precise movements, performance, and position on the court or on the field in ways never before possible. At that level, minute precision is the difference between sitting on the bench and winning a championship. Team managers can analyze team behavior and position in real time in ways that were never possible. A.I. can then even offer recommendations. Sports trainers and physical therapists can use motion capture cameras to detect minute imperfections in posture, motion, and repetition in rehabilitation exercises; injured athletes can mend better and faster. So students who are drawn to the world of exercise science, nutrition, sports management, and physical education use their understanding of Computer Science to help athletes develop.

The Beach:
Image and video processing can be used to analyze Drone footage of the surf at a public beach, looking for rip currents, sharks, or jellyfish. Erosion and pollution can be identified in areas not

accessible before. So students who are drawn to the world of outdoor public safety can use their understanding of Computer Science to make our world a better and safer place.

Automotive:
Self-driving cars can make transportation dramatically more safe, more efficient, with fewer traffic jams, faster arrivals, and fewer accidents. Cars today can adjust fuel/air mixtures and control brakes to avoid dangerous situations. So students who are drawn to the world of automotive technology can use their understanding of Computer Science to help people move in the world around them in safer and more economical ways.

Medicine:
Robot instruments can assist in surgery with accuracy and precision simply not possible with the human hand. Drones can deliver medical supplies to inaccessible areas after natural disaster. Instructions could be transmitted to the users. Miniature cameras can be inserted into the body for live video feed, images, virus identification, or organ analysis. So students who are drawn to the world of medicine can use their understanding of Computer Science to help people.

Computer Science is everywhere in the real world. You knew these things were possibly happening, but you may not have necessarily realized that CS was the reason.

Computer Science in the classroom

Ok, so now you have some feel for what Computer Science looks like in the world and you even explored a simple Hour of Code, but what does all of this look like with a teacher and a classroom full of students? How do we take such a broad topic and bring it into something real in the classroom for students to byte (heehee) into?

Students might write a beginner level interactive "game" around the concepts and vocabulary of predator, prey, and the food chain. I will suggest several beginner level block-based programs later in the book that are especially effective CS learning tools for younger students. This is important because we can introduce some of the basic CS constructs and concepts through games. The content of the game can be adjusted to fit anything you like. In general, the code will be the same.

For example, students understand that if you can get over 20000 points in a game on level 1, that you can get a bonus of 5000 points and also advance to level 2.

```
if ( score > 20000  &&  level == 1)
        {
                score = score + 5000;
                level = level + 1
        }
```

Your first lines of code! The above code, called a conditional statement, uses Boolean algebra, but it also involves incrementing a variable. This one piece of the project introduced and reinforced three concepts. Many teachers know that there is an energy and engagement that is part of games that is hard to capture in the traditional classroom; imagine the energy when they create their own games! That is why games are part of early (and even advanced) education in Computer Science.

The same code they learned making that game in high school might be used to handle a section of a professional-grade flight simulator used to train pilots, or a surgery simulator used to train doctors.

Pretty cool, huh?

 Another example might be for a student to program a robot to follow a track, much like an Amazon warehouse robot or a driverless car. Imagine a sheet of white poster board with a black "road" drawn across it. The students can access the two sensors on the bottom of the robot. One is on the left and the other on the right. Students can play with it to see what the readings are when the sensor sees a black line or white. They can collaborate on how they might program the robot to be able to stay on the black line, much like a person walking along the edge of a sidewalk. Any time either of the sensors detects black (that means it is off track), it turns the other direction and advances a bit. If both sensors "see" white then that means the robot is in the road, so they can tell it to move forward slightly

```
if (sensor.left = white AND sensor.right = white) THEN
        robot.forward()

if (sensor.left = black AND sensor.right = white) THEN
        robot.right(15)

if (sensor.left = white AND sensor.right = black ) THEN
        robot.left(15)
```

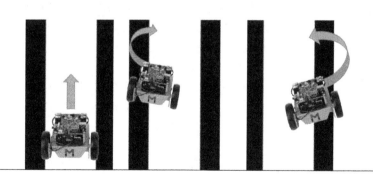

In an advanced class, students might try to run simulations such as a traffic intersection to determine optimum light timings. Or students might write an app for their smartphone to keep track of race event results at a track meet. One of our top volleyball students wrote an app to keep track of the statistics of her team. Students might find a local business with a mediocre website, redesign it and "give" it to the owner. Or they might create a food ordering system for a local restaurant. One group created a music playing program with only audio - no screen - for blind people using the human body as the "instrument." Students program their own functions in Minecraft that can actually be used the game. One girl made an app for women to use during self-examinations for breast cancer that would even text the results to her doctor. One of our boys made a to-do list all voice-controlled for soldiers wounded in battle who have limited arm movement. These apps were all created by students.

Does that sound like something your students would enjoy? Do the skills needed to do those projects seem like they would be valued in the world?

> *We don't expect all students to major in Computer Science and work at Microsoft or Google. Neither do we expect all students to be poets or museum curators, but yet they take classes in language and history. In the same way that students study math and science to help understand and contribute to the world around them, we also need students to be in command of the technology of industry and business and research.*

So hopefully you are starting to see what Computer Science is, how and where it exists in the real world, and even starting to envision having it at your school.

If this is true for you, you are **READY** *to* **ROCK**. Let's start designing your Computer Science program.

Section Two:

Ready to Rock
Ready to Change

This section is for the person who already understands what Computer Science is *and* is interested in actually implementing a class or program at his/her school. Perhaps you already are experienced in the CS classroom, but are just not getting the level of engagement and energy that you know could be there. Maybe your new principal has challenged you to increase the number of students in the CS classes. Or maybe you are just looking for new approach to teaching using project-based learning.

- What are some of the obstacles you are going to face?
- What are the common pitfalls you can avoid?
- What proven successes you can take advantage of?
- What are the advantages and limitations of different technologies?
- What style of class fits you, your school, and your students?
- How can you teach a Computer Science class if you are not a Computer Science "expert?"
- What technologies really engage students and how do you create learning experiences out of technology project?
- How can you take advantage of your super-high tech students?

   .....and ultimately the big question

- How can project-based learning transform your classroom?

Getting Started

School District tools for starting CS

Check out this success story:
www.youtube.com/watch?v=POiMh0qISpI

There is an excellent tool called SCRIPT to help lead you through some of the initial considerations, discussions, and questions for your leadership team. The CSFORALL initiative is an excellent resource and has created this tool to lead you through several of the crucial steps of bringing CS into your school. It's a great place to start. You can read more information about this here: http://advocate.csteachers.org/2017/11/08/use-the-script-to-develop-your-districts-own-csforall-plans/

Finding and recruiting students

This is an interesting topic. Build your program to attract anyone and everyone. Computer Science is not for the elite, and it's not just for the high-techy gurus.

CS programs in their early stages will have to work hard to generate interest from people that might not normally be attracted. Your hard core techies are probably already involved at your school and will be there to help you get the program off the ground, but I will encourage you _not_ to build your program towards that hard core techie audience. WHAT??!! Early on you want a program that all students can see themselves being part of. When people look inside the window of the CS classroom, they want to see people they can relate to in there. If your class is full of only one type of student, then that is what you are going to attract. Work hard to get females in your program. Work hard to get athletes. Work hard to get theatrical performers and musicians. Work hard to get poets. Work hard to get cheerleaders. Work hard to get your history lovers, science lovers, and foreign language lovers. That is important on several levels.

The technology industry has been dominated by one type of person for decades. So that means that most of the hardware, software, gadgets, and services that we use now have been through brainstorming, design, implementation, testing, and marketing--but with a very narrow single-sided lens. Of course, there have been people of diversity and women involved, but they seldom get any credit for their participation. As we get more diverse, we are going to be asking different questions with different priorities, different observations, different desires, different perceptions, and different passions; that translates to seeing our current products transform into better products. We will see new and different products we never thought about before. We will see another technology revolution larger and more powerful than ever before. And it starts in your school. We want your kids prepared to be a part of making this happen, instead of standing on the sidelines watching the world go by.

As your program starts to grow, make sure your assignments and projects are not gender-targeted. For example, if you were going to have students learn to code through making a game, don't assume everyone loves to have loud sound effects and stuff getting blown up by missiles. That is a very boy-centric inaccurate stereotype. In the same spirit, don't assume that your girls will all like a storytelling environment. These stereotypes are what we have to dismantle in our classroom. This is yet another reason to let students choose their own projects. Students can learn skills and demonstrate skills in the context of a variety of topics. You can give them the high level topic (for example a game that addresses a serious world issue, an app that addresses the needs of a physically-handicapped person, a program which simulates a real word scenario such as a retail business.) What you'll find is that through these assignments and projects, your students will connect with the discipline, but also start to look at CS as another tool they can use to express their ideas. That is what is most important in your early classes at this level.

When you have speakers, make sure they represent a wide variety of people from different genders, religions, cultures, and backgrounds. If you have girls in your class, have a female speaker. You want your female students to see a successful businessperson that they can relate to. Your speakers do not need to be high-level executives; you can invite recent graduates of college, "middle management", or a new owner of a company. But you do need to get speakers in your classroom (Skype, in person, on the phone, or whatever)

As you decorate the walls of your classroom, make sure you have images of people who look like the people you are trying to attract into your classes. In the examples and stories, you use in class discussions, make sure to use names and job titles that reflect the same diversity and equity as you are seeking in the population of your classes. When you praise students in class, make sure students see a wide variety of diversity in the recognitions.

These may seem like insignificant things to do, but trust me--they work and they are hugely important.

Take advantage of your elite tech students

Every class is going to have those kids who are amazing already and also quick and eager learners who don't need hand-holding. Embrace them, give them extra projects, give them freedom to explore, let them figure things out for you. But challenge them to go far beyond wherever they are. Let their project be collaborative, real world. Reach out to the local college or even local business to partner with them on some cool research projects. Let them research something for you, demonstrate or even teach the class. Encourage those advanced students to take an online class *during* your class time. Let them work on a project creating something for a fellow teacher or develop an app for the Android or Apple marketplace. For example: our daily class schedule rotates every day, so a student created a mobile-phone app (used by hundreds of people every day) that displays the correct daily sequence. A group of kids asked if they could put on their own CTF Cyber event. It took them months to plan and execute. The event was incredibly well received. These students will help you evaluate new technologies, research languages, test equipment, build better projects, even help you teach classes. If you make them take your intro CS curriculum, you've lost them. One approach we are using, because the advanced student is becoming more common, is an "Independent Study" proposal. Students who have specific projects already in mind can submit a two-three page application to be considered for a formal Independent study class. They still attend CS class, but they work on their own project. We will even have formal weekly check-in meetings to decide deadlines and evaluate progress results. Take advantage of this awesome energy.

Whole school approach

The primary goal of your K-12 CS program is to help students find inspiration to see the worth and value of Computer Science. We need CS to be part of regular academic conversation. It has to be considered a viable part of their education just as science, math or history. Make sure to include CS grades in GPA calculations and in award and recognition criteria. Include CS in any lists of subjects that students publically see. Use CS in any conversations the same way we might refer to any other "core" class. Students have to perceive that the school considers it exactly as they would any subject, requiring the same time and effort commitment, with the same value. It's not just "computer class." In that spirit, you might stop using the word "non-core", "elective", "special", or "term" course--or whatever vocab traditionally is used that gives a sense of "not as important." You will need your college counseling department to buy into your program as well. If they are not supporting it, students and parents will not respond to it. CS should not be a "special" class that students take to enrich their lives. In the same ways that language, math, and history are fundamental building blocks of the educated person, we must also look at CS.

Getting trained

There are lots of ways to get trained depending on the type of class you want to design at your school, the type of learner *you* are, what skills you already have, and when you have time.

One easy and fast way to get started is to take advantage of the already available resources-line. These types of resources include numerous YouTube video tutorial series (made by industry professionals and hobbyist), free on-line classes, and paid on-line class classes. Sites such as Udacity, Udemy, Alison, Coursera, EdX, and Code Academy are heavily used by millions of educators all over the world. On these sites, you can literally search whatever language you're interested in and find *free* (or *dirt cheap*) classes that you can begin **immediately**. These sites cater to anyone from the complete beginner to the advanced learner.

Kahn Academy, the "homework help" site actually has some excellent Computer Science training tutorials. Additionally, M.I.T. has made several of their introductory Computer Science classes available to the public in a program called MIT Open Courseware.

CODE.ORG facilitates training (free of charge) to teachers (elementary, middle, and high) who are interested in using their curriculum. Tens of thousands of teachers have gone through this training. This page (https://code.org/files/PL-Program-for-Me.pdf) can help you figure out which workshop you should attend, then you can find a workshop near you: https://code.org/educate/professional-learning

Microsoft has some excellent beginner level "classes" especially for elementary and middle school teachers *(but that also be used in the classroom with students)* in other disciplines to help learn all about CS. It includes numerous hands on practice activities.

> Using Physical computing and Micro-bit:
> https://education.microsoft.com/courses-and-resources/courses/physical-computing-and-its-role-in-education
>
> Using Minecraft: https://education.microsoft.com/courses-and-resources/courses/unleashing-creativity-with-makecode-and-minecraftee

The College Board maintains a list of approved workshops available for high school level CS teachers: http://eventreg.collegeboard.org/calendar-ap

Every year, new summer programs are offered, so this list is just a sampling from their site:

> Ria Galanos: Walton Summer Institutes. Ria is one of the most active members of the CS community.
> Rob Shultz: Western Kentucky University offers beginner and advanced workshops.
> Carleton Summer Teaching Institute
> AP Summer Institute
> AP Seminars Silicon Valley
> APCS: Maria Litvin: Her textbook is used by many teachers across the US. http://www.skylit.com/courses.html

Scholarships for high school AP teacher training

AP Fellows is an annual competitive grant program that provides AP Summer Institute scholarships for teachers at high schools serving minority or low-income students who have been traditionally underrepresented in AP courses. The $1,000 scholarships cover the cost of APSI tuition; any remaining funds may be applied to travel and expenses.

AP Rural Fellows is an annual competitive grant program that provides AP Summer Institute scholarships for teachers serving in rural areas of the country. The $1,500 scholarships cover APSI tuition; any remaining funds may be applied to travel and expenses.

Professional Development

Conferences and workshops are where you will get your best energy, ideas, and connections. Do everything you can to get to at least one every year. There are state, regional level, and national level gatherings.

Un-conferences, Teach Meets, and EdTech meetups can be as powerful as any national level events. Even consider putting one on at your school; you will be amazed at the response. The great thing about this type of event is that other than organizing the time and place, the event happens on its own! Just a quick explanation: The unconference model strategy is designed such that the people who attend will identify and choose the breakout sessions for the conference. This structure allows for the passions and trends of the group to be the focus. These are also great for in-school professional development days. Contact me for details on how to run an unconference!

Presenting at a workshop or conference of any size is an unbelievable experience. The process of completing an application and submission itself is a tremendously worthwhile process. It really makes you define what you do, how you do it, why you do it, and communicate why you think it's working. Don't worry about being the expert on something, but more so exploring interesting pedagogy, technology, or projects. Your audience just wants to hear about what you are doing, how you are doing it, results you've seen, things you've learned, changes you'll make. Presenting gives you confidence, is a great learning experience in itself, is a nice resume filler, and is great PR for you, your school, district, and city. It gives you credibility when you reach out to other educators

Here are some of the leading technology, Computer Science, and project-based learning conferences:

CSTA (https://www.csteachers.org) conference is for K-12 teachers of Computer Science. In July every year, it is a two-day conference with an additional two days of pre-workshop classes. Excellent for beginners as well as advanced teachers. Lots of scholarships available

SIGCSE Technical Symposium is in February each year and is the largest computing education conference worldwide organized by ACM SIGCSE.

Grace Hopper Celebration is a multi-day women-in-technology focused conference sponsored by all the big names in technology.

CUE Annual Conference is hosted in California and features hands-on workshops, technological exhibits, seminars, keynote speeches from respected speakers in the educational technology industry.

SXSWedu has over 14,000 attendees, 1,000 speakers, and 400 sessions. This conference tends to focus on new and innovative technologies

Serious Play conference is in July each year and has speakers from around the world related to game-based education, creating, and using games in the classroom

PBL World in California is the premier conference for project-based learning

Deeper Learning Conference in California is a gathering of innovative and inspiring educators and lots of hands-on through interactive workshops

BETT is the world's largest EdTech conference and is located in London. While it is an educational technology conference, there are numerous CS sessions.

NCCE conference is the largest Ed Tech conference in the northwest. While it is an educational technology conference, there are numerous CS sessions.

FETC regional conference is second largest educational conference on the east coast in the country. Although its focus is technology in the classroom, there are usually numerous Computer Science sessions.

ISTE conference is the largest in the country. Although it is a technology-in-the-classroom conference, there are usually numerous Computer Science sessions that are part of a CS track.

Converting technology class to CS

Some schools already have a "technology" class that focuses on non-CS topics such as word processing, spreadsheets, movie making, desktop publishing, and (ugh...gasp!) keyboarding. Take advantage of that time to introduce CS. Especially if you are unsure of exactly how to do that, using this already-planned-for time will give you a safe place to explore and experiment with a short module. Your students will love it, even if you are not an expert. In fact, in most cases, the students enjoy the chance to help you figure things out. If you go down this path, you may get push-back from parents, fellow teachers, and even students who confuse CS with computer applications. "Where else will they get their technology skills?" they will ask. As you start to understand what true Computer Science is and its value to your students, you will develop your own arguments. I guess for now, just blame it on me. Also, tell them to read this book when you are done.

Partnering with the I.T. department
(aka: The battle with I.T.)

If you talk with any teacher in any subject area that heavily uses technology, you will hear stories of software not running, websites blocked, installation issues, policy restrictions, permission problems, and compatibility struggles. Computer Science, by definition, is going to be your biggest headache if you do not address this head on. If students have their own devices and they can control what is on them, that will help, but if they are using school-supported devices, then you are going to have to have conversations with the I.T. department beforehand. Especially in a public school setting where districts determine policy and protocol, there has to be a system in place that handles the CS classes differently. Perhaps the computers run on a separate subnet, or they have a different set of network policy. Pretty much everything the kids are going to do is going to cause problems. I know it's not popular, but your best bet is to have a lab, or laptop set, that the teacher has true control over as administrator. Yes, that person will need to be trained for proper procedures, protocols, and reviews, but you have to give that teacher *trust, room to grow*, room to experiment, and security permissions to install, access, and approve. There are so many programming languages, and so many ways to program in all those languages, it is sometimes hard to determine everything beforehand. In general, we find if you can find web-based solutions, those are somewhat better than installed, but still not perfect. The virus protection software may also have issues with executing software designed by students. If you do not address this up front, it will likely cause problems for your teacher. Having the I.T. involved and supporting the CS program will have huge benefits. In fact, the I.T. department can help teach the classes as speakers, project leaders, and as resources for research and exploration. One approach you might even try is *instead of fighting them...join them*! Invite I.T. into your classroom. Let them teach a couple days in your class. Take the kids on a field trip to see the network and server rooms. The more they support what you do, they less obstacles there will be. Later in the book, I'll share some success stories from fellow teachers across the country. For example, one teacher in Washington, DC makes sure everything they use in the classroom is available online so every student has access offsite, but it also works well in the classroom because there are no installs.

Who can teach CS classes?

So these tend to be from several different groups:

- Actual Computer Science educators who are trained in CS and have experience in the classroom
- Teachers of other subject areas who love technology and interested in trying
- Teachers of other subject areas who get thrown into the CS teaching gig and do not have any experience
- Folks from the business world who leave business to come into education

Ideally, people in the first group are your first choice, but just because they are in that category does not necessarily mean they are the best teachers. But it does mean that they can probably jump in quicker and even hit the ground running. These are the teachers who might be willing to develop their own curriculum and develop an entire sequence and programs for your school or district

The second group is sometimes my favorite. Especially in your intro classes, this person can handle those classes as long as they are given room & time to explore, fail, explore, and ultimately find what works. This person could easily handle an elementary, middle school, or even a class even as high as the AP CS Principles class. For the AP CS class, you might need a more skilled faculty. I say this because there are numerous resources available for this type of person. For this level of expertise, their desire and willingness to do it is what is important. There are several proven effective curricula for all grade levels that I'll discuss later in the book.

The third group is not necessarily a negative. It just means it might be your least confident group. The good thing is they understand teaching and classroom management and how to run a class in general. For this level, as long as they can keep a couple weeks ahead, there is enough excellent curricula that they can use. For this person, just getting used to the programming language, software used to code, and the technology itself is the number one issue. A few workshops or on-online classes might be all that is needed. This person will also need leads on connecting with the larger CS community for ideas and advice.

The fourth group can be a gold mine depending on where you are. Take the time to research the area you live it and figure out what industries exist that would value CS education. Keep in mind, most industries have IT and technology as part of their business, so don't limit yourself to only technology companies. Reach out to them and see if there is interest in them being part of your classes as mentors and teachers. Even if they can only offer one or two times per week, it can help. This the essence of the TEALS program (for high school).

> TEALS: This program works with the local business community to bring in locally qualified professionals to partner with a teacher at the school to team-teach AP CS. The program has helped 1,000+ high schools across the U.S. build and grow teacher capacity to teach high school computer science. For some schools, this might provide that starting point for you. tealsk12.org/schools.

What are the attributes of the successful project-based CS teacher?

Besides technology, engineering, or programming experience, and a "tinkering" passion, what are some of the personal attributes that would be advantageous in this position? Obviously, no one person will possess all of these qualities, but these descriptors can be one tool to help find good people.

- Embraces that there is never a single answer to CS challenges
- Has a hands-on approach for students, and a hands-off approach by the teacher
- Has the ability to step back and let students figure things out
- Has the ability to let failure happen
- Has the ability to let learning happen on its own, without necessarily "telling" the students
- Has the ability to bring the real world into the classroom through projects, examples, field trips, videos, books, movies, speakers, and assignments.
- Is always experimenting and exploring with technology
- Is eager to embrace new technologies
- Is willing to *not* be the expert in the room at all times
- Accepts that curriculum will dynamically change every year

Hiring Part 1

This is going to be one of your school's biggest challenges. Hiring is different than in most other disciplines, even more so than the traditional hard-to-find math and science disciplines. And there are reasons why:

The demand for people who understand technology in these ways is *huge* in BUSINESS and INDUSTRY. That means that business and industry are going to be going after the same people you are. They will be able to offer salaries and benefits that you cannot. And many will fall prey to that. Keep in mind not everyone is motivated only by money. This is a crucial understanding and might be your bargaining chip.

An interesting opportunity is finding folks who have already been part of the extremely grueling and demanding 24/7/365 high tech business world. They might be tiring of that and eager to still be involved, but just not in business. The idea of working with kids and cool tech toys might be exactly what they need. What you are offering might just be what sounds enticing to them. I would embrace this as a tremendous opportunity. When you meet people in the community, reach out and connect.

One of the additional battles that may not be on your radar yet, but is still there, concerns diversity. You do not want all of your CS teachers to be Caucasian males. You want your CS program to be attractive to women, people of color, and people of various cultures and religions. This will help to attract additional students into your program and also open up a huge potential recruitment market.

Hiring part 2: Think out of the box

The most highly qualified teachers are going to have their choice. You are going to have to pay for experience and proven success. This increased pay requirement may or may not line up with your standard pay scale. Keep in mind you might have to pay more for a CS teacher than a history or English teacher. You can also consider additional compensation ideas.

Get creative and think out of the box. CS folks love their technology and might be enticed to your school in other ways. These folks love learning about new technologies, software, and hardware. Provide a budget for exploration of new technologies.

Other compensation motivators can be offering Professional Development funds to go to the top conference and attend workshops. Provide funds that can be used to explore new technologies for their classroom. Give them time off to visit other schools and businesses to get ideas. Make sure teachers have current and leading edge computers for their own use in the classroom. It's not wasted money those technologies might be the next wave and your school will be at the forefront. Computer science curriculum needs to change from time to time. It is important that teachers are regularly given the opportunity to modify the contents of a course, create new courses, or even remove existing courses.

For example: at my school, we were able to hire a highly qualified person who had never before been given freedom in the classroom to explore his own ideas and develop his own curriculum. So while we could not offer the salary he probably deserved, we were able to offer quality of classroom-life and room to explore. Over time, we were able to do better on salary and we have seen that teacher become one of the most innovative Computer Science teachers on the east coast.

Many of these highly qualified prospective teachers may be tempted by business to work part-time. Be flexible and consider offering time off to partner with business in the community, possibly as a side job or just work on projects. That might help keep those teachers in your classroom because they can make extra income on the side with their tech skills.

The Silo Effect

In some schools, there will be only a single CS teacher, which means that teacher will not have regular colleagues to bounce things off, test ideas, get feedback, and to collaborate with. Do not underestimate the importance of that. Some schools put CS under business, math, CT or even IT departments…which means that you have a teacher in a department that does not value them or have any connection. That can bring as much division as unity. Determining where CS fits is something you should not take lightly. Consider letting CS be its own discipline. Long term this will provide you with more opportunities.

In this spirit, you will need to provide professional development funds for your CS faculty to go to workshops and conferences, because in some cases, that might be the only collegiality they get. They are going to need those networking opportunities to form partnerships that are crucial to their own professional development--especially early on. Administrators: support that in whatever way you can--it is incredibly important, especially if you have a small number of CS teachers. Find out what conference they'd like to go to and *send them*. Most states have active CSTA (K-12 Computer Science Teachers Association) chapters, so sending your teachers gives them an excellent chance to meet people. If your state's chapter is not as strong, perhaps there is opportunity to take the lead with getting the chapter off the ground. There are several very active social media options, list-serves and discussion groups around Computer Science Education. We will list some later in the book.

Teachers: This is something you do not want to take for granted. This idea of feeling *on-your-own* is real; lots of Computer Science teachers know it well. Take advantage of the PD money and time your school offers you to attend these workshops and conferences at least once per year. Another excellent idea is to put on your own conference. It can be rejuvenating just getting people together to talk about ideas, share successes and failures, and compare notes about curriculum. You'll be amazed at the response you get.

CS Networking

Following are several national level organizations and initiatives you can connect with. It is vital to get connected in whatever ways you can. In this book, I'll give you numerous opportunities for those connections.

Computer Science for All
Former president Barack Obama, in partnership with industry leaders created a Computer Science in education initiative and dedicated millions of dollars! The Trump administration has pledged to continue this investment. You are definitely going to want to read more about. It is an amazing source of resources, advice, information, and community called *Computer Science for All* https://obamawhitehouse.archives.gov/blog/2016/01/30/computer-science-all

CSTA: This is the leading K-12 Computer Science Teachers Association which provides networking and support for thousands of CS teachers largely in the US, but the international community is really starting to grow rapidly. http://www.csteachers.org/ . There are two ways to connect: the national organization that members will join in order to be part of their local chapters. Most large cities have active chapters that can be of tremendous value to both new and

veteran teachers. Every year, they put on the only Computer Science conference especially for teachers.
http://www.csteachers.org/page/2018Conference

SIGCSE http://sigcse.org/sigcse/ (The Special Interest Group for Computer Science Education)
This group is under the umbrella of ACM (Association of Computing Machinery.) The scope of SIGCSE is to provide a global forum for educators to discuss research and practice related to the learning, and teaching of computing, the development, implementation, and evaluation of computing programs, curricula, and courses at all education levels, as well as broad participation, educational technology, instructional spaces, and other elements of teaching and pedagogy related to computing. This group tends to be skewed more towards higher education, but they do have active high school teacher members. SIGCSE's flagship conference is held annually: http://sigcse.org/sigcse/events/symposia

ISTE: International Society for Technology in Education. This organization continues to grow every year. It's not a Computer Science based organization, but it embraces all aspects of technology in education, and we are seeing CS become more of a part. Every summer, there is a huge conference with 15,000+ people, and there is usually a CS track with some good presentations. They also provide technology standards, including a new CS section.

CS Publications

beanz: is an excellent print and online magazine. While it is targeted towards upper elementary age and even middle school age, it has excellent articles and interesting perspectives on a huge variety of languages and technologies. www.kidscodecs.com.

Hello World: A free magazine for computing teachers and digital making educators. It's produced as a collaboration between the Raspberry Pi Foundation, the British Computer Society and Computing At School, but content is as relevant to US based educators as to those in the UK. Lesson activities and features are written by educators, for educators.

CSTA Weekly digest: **Computer Science Today:**
http://multibriefs.com/optin.php?CSTAORG

CSTA quarterly newsletter: **The Voice:**
https://www.csteachers.org/general/custom.asp?page=CSTAVoice

AP Computer Science : One of the most active online discussion and question-asking forum for Computer Science.: https://apcommunity.collegeboard.org/group/apcompsci/discussion-boards

For those that want to take a deep dive into the publication world, there are many more specialized Computer Science, Engineering, and similar publications you might want to check out: http://sigcse.org/sigcse/resources/publish

CS on Facebook

These social media forums are especially good for discussions, partnerships, and interesting ideas around CS. Each discussion group has unique perspectives and strengths, and most of the members of the groups are especially vocal and opinionated. It's a highly intelligent audience, so be prepared to be challenged and questioned about your ideas. Great for feedback about projects and curriculum.

AP CS
https://www.facebook.com/groups/APComputerScienceTeachers/

AP Principles
https://www.facebook.com/groups/1029824640390220/

CS Education Discussion
https://www.facebook.com/groups/CSEdForum/

CS Education and Research
https://www.facebook.com/groups/1546763215587966/

Computer Science Educators
https://www.facebook.com/groups/cptrscied/

Computer Science Teachers Association
https://www.facebook.com/groups/FollowCSTA/

College Board AP Community
https://apcommunity.collegeboard.org/

What technologies, languages, and devices should you use?

The great news is the there is no wrong answer here. What are your passions? What are the passions of students? What community partnerships can you find? How much money in your budget? If hardware is your thing, go in that direction. Love app design? Then go that route. Robots are interesting to you? Excellent, let them be part of your program. Love the "maker-space world?" Your kids will love it, and *yes*, it does make sense in context of what we are talking about here. Got some gamers in class? Let them make their own games. Take advantage of the energy around technology to let your parents and students help you research and explore your options.

There are so many technologies, languages, and devices available…many of these can accomplish the same things. Here is a partial list of technologies just to get the conversation started and your mind wandering
.

> ***NOTE: New technologies come onto the market every few months. They all have many things in common, and each offers something unique. Most of the following devices have been available for at least a couple years, but no guarantee they will continue. My goal is more to show a sampling of the kinds of technologies you can use. I recommend experimenting with several of these (or others like them) to see what works best in your class. Your passions should be reflected in the technologies you use in your classroom***

Robots: *(Robots are one of the most engaging technologies you can use in any age classroom)*
- NO MONEY? No Problem: There are online "robot" simulators you can use as well. This is one such free downloads for Windows with lots of tutorials and educator resources. http://www.robotbasic.org/
- No room for Robots? There are several relatively cheap alternatives that allow 100% online robotics simulators + curriculum. Here is an example: for about $300, you can get a full classroom "set" including curriculum. The kits allows you

to design your robotics, program them, and also run them virtually in different environments. http://www.robotvirtualworlds.com/

Got room? Got money? Most of the following educational robots run $100-$200 each and have block-based programming environments for beginners/younger kids. Many of them also have text-based programming as well for more advanced students.

(E)lementary age, (M)iddle school age, (H)igh school age

- LEGO WeDO2.0(E,M): Excellent choice for younger kids. Lots of STEM curriculum. Because of the "building"  element that LEGO brings, this series can be used for years in different ways. The coming together of the building and the coding a blend of engineering and programming, which is an excellent combination that allows you to reach a wider audience.

- LEGO Mindstorm EV3 block programming(E,M). Great kits with tons of Legos, wheels, gears, Bluetooth, and sensors. Very popular. LEGO EV3 with RobotC(M,H): Great kits with tons of Legos, wheels, gears, Bluetooth, and sensors. Advanced text-based programming language for your more advanced programmers.

- Thymio(M,H). Sturdy robot with accelerometer, seven infrared object sensors, two line detectors, tons of lights, buttons, remote control, and sounds. Can also be used to draw using a marker.
Page 50

Take advantage of the pen hole to let kids "draw" with it. No matter the age, they always love the art part. A cheaper version of this style of robot is made by another company and is called the Edison, which offers some of the same capabilities.

- Finch(M,H) Check out their free "loaner" program for a class set. Includes a 15 ft. USB cable but I think they have a wireless option. Can be programmed using your choice of over 12 languages, both block-based for beginners and advanced text-based languages. Sturdy robot with accelerometer, two infrared object sensors, a nose light, the ability to talk and access internet. Lots of curriculum on their website for all age levels.

- Ozobot(E) Great introductory robot uses line followers and color code detection. Evo(older kids) and Bit(younger kids) models have proximity or optical sensors. Lots of curriculum on their site.

…and even more cool gadgets…

- **Vidcode**: www.vidcode.com : Students 4th - 12th graders use code-based video editing as the medium to actually learn how to code. This is a really out-of-the-box approach, but will keep your kids engaged, especially those who love the arts. They have converted to a paid model, but this still might be worth checking out! Students actually code video special-effects, Snapchat and Instagram-inspired filters, memes and more! Full curriculum provided, including AP Principles.

- **Microsoft MakeCode** https://makecode.com/ : This site needs to be something you check out. It works with several technologies such as Micro-bit, Circuit Playground, Minecraft, and Cue robots. All of these are dirt cheap, and the site uses block-based coding as well as JavaScript text based, so it can handle beginners all the way to advanced. Teachers who use this site LOVE IT. There is also a great educator community around this that you can tap into. A great place to start for your elementary and middle schools.

  - (part of MakeCode) **Minecraft** (E, M): free. Students can program and see the results of their code executed right there in the game itself. Microsoft owns Minecraft and Minecraft.edu and has provided lots of  resources, community, and tutorials.

  - (part of MakeCode) **Microbit** (E,M): The software is free but the boards themselves are $15 each. This is really cool! Incredibly cheap all-in-one handheld computing device with accelerometer, compass, 25 LED lights, buttons, Bluetooth, lots of room for add-ons. Your  elementary and middle school kids will absolutely love this. For a teacher, it's pretty easy to use and get started. Lots of resources, project ideas, and tutorials online.

- (part of MakeCode) **Adafruit Playground Express** (E,M): the software is free but the boards are $20 each. This device is *really* cool!  Incredibly cheap all-in-one handheld computing device with motion sensors, ten colored LED lights, temperature, sound, buttons, Bluetooth, lots of room for add-ons. A bit more advanced than Microbit. Lots of resources, project ideas, and tutorials online.

- **Arduino and Raspberry Pi** (M,H)
  This is probably the thing I am most excited because of the tremendous capabilities this offers. It is easy to extend and add on endlessly and cheaply. These mini "computers" are less than $50 for a kit which has everything you'll need to get started, including several sensors and all wires. Most kits also include easy to follow tutorials and instructions. It is probably 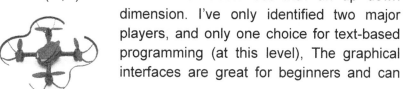 not going to be good for real beginners, so you might do this with higher level kids. It comes with several sensors students can use: Motion, Press, Temperature, GPS, Light, color, ultrasonic, water, magnet, shock, tilt, humidity, etc. There are "starter kits" that come with everything you need to get started. I recommend spending $30 and exploring this on your own to get a feel for it. I could see this becoming a much larger component of our curriculum.

- **Drones** (M,H): These are like robots but with an up down dimension. I've only identified two major players, and only one choice for text-based programming (at this level), The graphical interfaces are great for beginners and can also be used (by teachers) to learn the nuances of programming drones. There is still lots of room for expansion and improvement in this market. While the energy around programming drones is awesome, they can be very finicky, so just be flexible and open minded. Regardless, your kids will really love it. These both cost about $100 each. The team at Robolink (CoDrone) are very passionate about CS and provide excellent support.

- Parrot Mambo (indoor, outdoor): Block based
- Codrone (indoor): Block based and text-based. We have a set of 15 of these indoor drones. These are what we use in our "drones" section of class.

- **Game Design** related instruments. You can never go wrong coding games in class. The energy around games is amazing. There are programs that can be used specifically for game design, and you can also just pick any language that you have experience with and use that or game design (i.e. Java, JavaScript, Python, C-Sharp, C++, and numerous other languages). You can use just the keyboard and mouse, but as students get better, you can start to explore peripheral devices such as :
  - Dance Pad((M,H))($40)
  - Controller joystick(M,H)($35)
  - Steering Wheel(M,H)($100)

- **Tablets and phones** (app design)(M,H): These are crucial if you want to develop Android apps or iPhone/iPad apps. Even though there are emulators that let you test apps "virtually," I recommend you get real tablets/phones for the full effect. This technology is great for writing apps that use touchscreen, accelerometer, GPS, maps, audio, camera, voice recognition. You can buy tablets cheap (Amazon Fire is $35), Samsung Tabs are $100+, lots of off-brands for $25. You can find old i-phones on Ebay. Kids of all genders and diversity really love app design. Highly recommended. We have lots of these.

- **3D Motion capture** camera for facial recognition, voice recognition, skeleton detection, voice recognition, object identification. In our classes, we use the old Kinect cameras for this. So while this model is no longer in production, the experience of using them is something we have had tremendous success with. This technology works with Scratch, Java(Processing), Python, or C-sharp. The projects are some of my favorites because it is true 3D program and uses a non-standard interface, which students need to get used it. The actual Kinect brand is no longer supported by Microsoft, but for the next few years, they will still be available to buy online through various vendors, craigslist, Ebay, etc. Some teachers have had some good success in middle school with the Scratch version, but we use the text-based coding in the high school. Note: I recommend using it with your advanced classes. It's a true 3D experience. This is one our most engaging technologies. My goal in using this is not to make students experts on this specific technology, but to interact with a non-traditional device in ways they are not used to. When they finally make their way into whatever industry, they will be confronted with technologies that are unknown. I want that experience to not be unfamiliar to them.

- **Mindwave** (detecting brain waves)(H): These are not really mind reading , but more so a wave detecting devices. There are five or six regular waves that the brain gives off that can be detected. The technology works with a variety of languages including Java or C. These are really cool, and definitely "out there", but I am listing it here just to get you to think OUT OF THE BOX. The ability to detect brain waves is awesome; each brainwave  corresponds to a certain type of behavior, so it does work and can be used as input! The goal of something like this is really just to get them interacting with non-traditional technologies that help them interpret and interact with the world around them differently. These cost around $100.

- **Mixed Reality, Augmented Reality, and Virtual Reality** headsets and hand controllers.(H):

Mixed reality has become the phrase that the industry is embracing that represents all of these devices. These would be for your more advanced classes if you want to actually build apps, but you can certainly demo them in class at any age. In fact, if you are looking for an engaging "recruitment tool", this is it! These range from $300 to $3000 and are all similar, but with their specific unique factors. Most use UNITY software to develop (free on both Mac and PC), so it would be for your more advanced classes. This field is growing and new units are coming onto the market regularly including HoloLens, Mira Lens, Meta 2, HTC Vive, Oculus Rift, Aer, Lenovo, Dell, HP, and Samsung. This technology is something you need to look at. It has the capability to transform education in ways we have not seen. It has the power to let people experience people, places, and events in ways simply not possible before. Preparing students now to be able to produce content just makes sense.

As you can see, there are many options...some obvious...others are out-of-the-box and even crazy. This is where being part of the CS community can be great to ask questions about and see what other teachers are using. I can't emphasize enough---You'll find these communities are some of the most engaged, helpful, and active communities in the educational world, *so get connected*!

Web-based tools

There are many great online resources where you or your students can go to explore programming. These sites come and go every year, so there is no guarantee, but the sites listed here have been around for at least a couple years. These sites listed are meant to be a sampling of what is available. You'll need to experiment to find the kind that works best in your classroom.

Many of these have pre-made challenges and tutorials, but *not necessarily* a full curriculum to follow. You could explore any of these in any age level classroom. I've used this style of site before, and what I found worked best was after you spend a few minutes showing how to get around the site, have each kid do a few of the tutorials and then have them either add on to those projects, or have them create their own from scratch. The following are proven and have been around a while, which means there are plenty of resources, community, project ideas, and tutorials. Some of these are beginner level block-based for and some are text-based for advanced learners.

- **App Lab**: https://code.org/educate/applab Great for all grade levels and grades to learn to develop smart phone apps.
- **Hour of Code**: https://code.org/learn Great for all levels and grades to learn how to make games, program apps, command robots, design websites, and numerous other "1-hour" lessons.
- **Scratch**: https://scratch.mit.edu/ Great for elementary and middle school to develop games and interactive entertainment
- **Tynker**: https://www.tynker.com/ Great as a "next step" for students after Scratch.

- **Code Monster** & Code Maven : http://www.crunchzilla.com/ A fun way to actually learn text-based coding. A kid-friendly interface actually leads students through code step by step.
- **Applnventor**: App development for Android and iPhone. Surprisingly powerful and relevant for beginner all the way to advanced. Highly recommended. There are lots of resources, project ideas, and tutorials online You can use the built in emulator, or connect to tablet or phone. **Thunkable** is a spin-off from AppInventor that might also be worth checking out.
- **Programmr**: http://www.programmr.com/ I love this site! It has a huge number of languages to choose from so students could even use this site as a place to explore languages. You can do mini-challenges in any language or take an entire class in Java, PHP, C++,Python, and C#.
- **Game Lab**: (COD.ORG) https://code.org/gamelab
  Game Lab is a programming environment where you can make simple animations and games with objects and characters that interact with each other. It's meant for younger kids elementary and maybe middle school Lots of tutorials and resources.

Downloaded programs

These products are proven effective and engaging tools for the classroom. And they have been around a long time which means there are lots of resources, tutorials, project ideas, and community to connect with.

- **Alice** 3D world(M,H): https://www.alice.org/ Outstanding tool made by Carnegie Melon that uses a 3D world to teach programming. Best suited for upper elementary, middle and high schoolers. It's designed to be story-telling like in nature, but it can be as advanced as needed. In fact, you can even "export" your code into actual Java; it could be used in an AP level course.

- **Kodu**(E,M): Kodu is a great beginner drag-n-drop 3D game development world especially useful in 3rd-6th grade. Through a game design set of tools, students can easily put together the components of an actual 3D game. It is a great introduction to CS concepts.
- **Scratch Jr.** Grades 1-3: beginner block-based simple game development. This is a great program for beginner game design.
- **Gamemaker**(M): Intermediate text-based game development. This program can be used in drag-n-drop mode or you can do text-based programming, so it can be beginner or advanced level. There are lots of tutorials and resources online. Additionally, it even has formal curriculum built based on it, for example (http://www.gameprogrammingcourse.com/)
- **Monogame**(H): advanced text-based game development
  This can be used to program games and applications for iOS or Windows or Android. It uses the language of C-Sharp, which is a common professional language. Students can design and code once and that can be translated into the different platforms when complete. It installs into Visual Studio(free). Lots of tutorials online.
- **PYGAME (H)** is an add-on to Python for doing game design. This is what we use in our 9th grade class. Lots of books and websites to help:

  https://inventwithpython.com/pygame/
  http://programarcadegames.com/

  You can also program games in PYTHON without any special add-on libraries. For example:
  http://www.pythonforbeginners.com/games/

  And also a good Python Youtube video series tutorials:
  https://www.youtube.com/watch?v=ujOTNg17LjI

- **Unity** (H): Intermediate 3D world and game development. This is one of the leading 2D and 3D game design and interactive program software. There is a learning curve, but once you get the hang of it, you can do amazing things with it. While it can be used to create beginner level games, it is also used to create some of the world's leading commercial level games.

Programming languages

Following are several languages used by many teachers across the country. This list is my no means complete; it is meant to communicate the kinds of options you can explore in your classroom. You will need to experiment to figure out what works best with your students.

Java: advanced text-based language. It's been around a long time and is one of the most common languages used. Many colleges have been using this language for decades. The AP CS curriculum is Java-based. It is not the best language for beginners. It can be used to make any type of software, app, simulation, or game. Eclipse, Jcreator, Greenfoot, BlueJ, and Dr. Java are all excellent and FREE programs you can use for JAVA. They are all used by teachers around the world and are all supported online with tons of tutorials and resources. There are thousands of resources online and in print related to Java.

JavaScript: a text-based scripting language used in browsers. This is an excellent choice of a language to study in class because there are tons of resources online, including numerous entire curriculum and even on-line classes. Students can use it to design web-based programs, games, and interactive web pages. You can use any text editor to program, but professionals use the free programs such as

Brackets, Notepad++, Sublime, Atom. These are all excellent and FREE programs you can use as well.

Python: This is an excellent language to learn because it is one of the top 10 languages in the world. Students can use it to program games, applications, simulations, and even mobile apps. You can just use the built-in IDLE to program that comes with Python(free), or you can use other programs that have some additional features: Pycharm, CodeSkulptor, and Wings are excellent programs.

HTML5/CSS: text-based language web-page design. These languages can be used to design webpages at a professional level, but can also be used in the classroom for simple website coding. HTML5, in addition to being used as a design language for webpages, can also be used for game design. Lots of resources online.

Swift: text-based language for app development. This language is not for beginners. It can be used to write apps for iPhone, iPad, and Mac products. Swift does not run on a PC; it requires a MAC. Swift is programmed using the free X-Code program. There is an iPad app called Playground that lets students explore simple Swift programming.

C++: advanced text-based language. Many colleges use this. It's been around a long time. Definitely not a beginner language. Tons of resources and tutorials online. Your students who are going into actual Computer Science might find value in learning this language, but otherwise it is probably not good as an introductory class.

C-Sharp, C#: A lot like Java, growing in popularity. You can use Visual Studio (free version) or Unity to program in this language. It can be used to create any software, simulation, or game. It could be used in a high school level class.

Visual Basic This is an older language, but is still used to design professional level software. Advanced students can use Visual Studio (free version) to program. It's graphical based and object-oriented with a blend of text-based coding. Lots of tutorials and resources online. It could be used in an introductory class as well as a more advanced one.

Small Basic is a great beginner tool that is an awesome way to introduce kids to an in-between block and text-based environment. There are actually over 200 "versions" of BASIC, one of the oldest languages there is. This is a relatively unknown product, but is really a well-supported, very useful, and easy entrance into programming and Computer Science. The interface is very kid-friendly. You can actually do some amazing things in this language.

Block-Based languages are really just *easy-to-use* interfaces that generate code "behind the scenes". It still allows students to learn constructs, commands, and skills—BUT it allows them to do so (almost) free from syntax. Syntax is basically the "structure" of typing things in correctly. One missed comma, semi-colon, or quote and nothing works. One misspelled command can cause other errors. This happens even in advanced classes, but it especially happens in the early days of learning how to program. There are several of these we have mentioned in the book already, such as Scratch Jr, Scratch, Mindstorm Lego, Tinker, Hopscotch, GameFroot, and Alice.

Online free advanced language editors

** **Extra Awesome Hint:** These allow you to program online in a variety of languages without having to install any software.

Tutorials point: http://www.tutorialspoint.com/codingground.htm

CodeChef: https://www.codechef.com/ide

Curriculum: ideas and implementation

Standards

Computer Science is a new field to the world of education and so our standards' journey has been like the Wild West. With the recent push for CS into schools, some states are starting to produce their own standards, so you need to check with your local CSTA chapter to see what the expectations are for the grades you teach. There are several curricula (listed in this book) you can use that are already researched and aligned with the CSTA standards.

Why is standardizing so hard in CS? Well, Computer Science is different from other subjects in that the content is so wide and vast that it is harder to determine what is part of an introductory first level class. For programs which have sequences of CS classes, it is hard to find consistency in the types of classes that are offered. There are so many relevant languages and technologies. There are many places where variation can occur...and this is a *good* thing. Based on the preferences, background, and experiences of your teachers and students and community, schools can take advantage of these distinctions to define their own program. Your goal is to get students into CS-- they can fine tune their learning in college--right now we just want to give them exposure and solid introduction to get them in the CS door. If one of your faculty has a medical background, maybe projects are directed towards the medical industry. If one of your faculty has a strong engineering background, then that program might have a heavy maker-space feel to it where students build their own computers and gadgets using Raspberry-Pi and ad hoc sensors. Awesome. There is no wrong direction here. Letting the passions of your faculty, as well as your students, be an integral part of the curriculum is vital.

Standards can also be a double-edged sword. Used correctly, they can be very effective in keeping your curriculum aligned with recommended skills and concepts and providing consistent age appropriate alignment with schools across the country. Standards help ensure there are no gaps in the curriculum and that there is a flow through the sequential classes both vertically and horizontally. There are incredible CS programs that are supported by both state and national CSTA standards. There are also programs which are so heavily focused on standards that they rip the life out of the class. In order to decide how to incorporate this into your program, it is important to decide what the goal of your CS classes is going to be. Part of that goal is going to be skills and concepts, so it is crucial that you identify what those targets are and make sure that they are part of your CS class. You should be familiar with age and grade level appropriate standards as you design your projects. However, do not let your standards drive the curriculum. What I mean by that is make sure your projects are real world, useful, meaningful, challenging, rigorous, and relevant FIRST. Then use the standards to support and enhance that project. Not the other way around. That will make more sense as you get into it.

CSTA:
https://www.csteachers.org/general/custom.asp?page=standards

ISTE:
https://www.iste.org/standards/for-computer-science-educators

Elementary School

In the push for Computer Science, most schools and districts look first to their high schools and then sometimes to their middle schools. But we have to go even lower. Our elementary school students LOVE IT, LOVE IT, LOVE IT. The tools, software, technologies, and energy around Computer Science for this age group are amazing. This natural engagement is extremely important as it helps CS be a regular part of education for students and parents. As they progress through the years, writing code will be as common as writing a paragraph or reading a story. Later in the end of book, you'll read about Dr. Julie Sessions' incredible experience of bringing CS into the lower grades. Later in the book, you'll also hear from librarian Julie Hembree about how she has made coding a regular part of learning for her students with tremendous success. Similar programs are popping up all over the place with amazing energy and incredible success, the kind of experience that makes your TEACHERS want to do it. There is tremendous opportunity in *younger* ages because there is less pressure from standardized testing, college admissions, and high school graduation process. Use this time to just let the kids explore technology, software, and hardware. Elementary school is when students still run to class because they are so excited. Embrace that energy. Let CS be what they run to.

Code.org has been one of the most active with teachers and students in this age group. They have created an entire curriculum (free) with lots of classroom management tools, lesson plans, tutorials, and community: https://code.org/educate/curriculum/elementary-school

Microsoft has a module that can be used in the classroom related to physical computing using the Micro-bit and Minecraft. It is for beginners and can be used in upper elementary ages. It's actually a great tool for the teacher to learn as well as the students.

https://education.microsoft.com/courses-and-resources/resources/handson-computing-with-microsoft-makecode

Middle School

If we wait until high school to begin Computer Science, we have missed the boat. Middle school is when students start to really develop connections with disciplines and find out what they are passionate about. We want Computer Science to be part of that experience. Don't believe me? Offer an "Hour of Code" one day after school or one evening and I bet 50-100 students show up! Computer Science needs to take its place as one of the many disciplines students explore and learn. Schools are deciding to make CS a priority and have included it in the academic day. At our school, which is probably just like your school, we have numerous middle schoolers doing high school level Computer Science already. Embrace that. Take advantage of that. Middle school is that place where students can really explore; why not let CS be one of the experiences they have?!

Following are several proven curricula used by many teachers across the country, but new programs arrive every year, so this list will be longer soon. This list is meant to communicate the kinds of options you will have available to you. You will need to experiment to figure out what works best in your program.

CS Discoveries:Code.org
https://studio.code.org/courses?view=teacher
Computer Science Discoveries is appropriate for 6-10th grade students and can be taught as a semester or yearlong introductory course (3-5 hours per week of instruction for 9+ weeks). The course takes a wide lens on computer science by covering topics such as programming, physical computing, HTML/CSS, and data. Students engage with computer science as a medium for creativity,

communication, problem solving, and fun. The course inspires students as they build their own websites, apps, games, and physical computing devices.

Small-Basic:
https://social.technet.microsoft.com/wiki/contents/articles/16299.small-basic-curriculum.aspx
Learn all about Small Basic by using the free curriculum. With the curriculum, you can learn about Small Basic in separate lessons - just like you would in a classroom. You can download the curriculum, which includes PowerPoint decks to teach from. As a teacher or as a student learning Small Basic on your own, the curriculum will guide you step by step.

Microsoft Middle School Micro-bit curriculum:
https://makecode.microbit.org/courses/csintro This course is written for teachers who may not have a Computer Science background, or who may be teaching an "Intro to Computer Science" course for the first time. This course takes approximately 14 weeks to complete, spending about 1 week on each of the first 11 lessons, and 3 weeks for students to complete the final project at the end. It uses the Micro-bit

https://makecode.microbit.org/courses/ucp-science   The **Science Experiments** lessons are designed help the student gain a greater understanding of the forces and behavior of the physical world. This is done using methods of observation, measurement, and data analysis. By incorporating the Micro-bit in the experiments, the lessons are a great way to teach both science and computing in the same activity.

CS Fundamentals: Code.org
https://studio.code.org/courses?view=teacher

Designed to be fun and engaging, Code.org's progression of CS Fundamentals courses blended online and "unplugged" non-computer activities to teach students computational thinking, problem solving, programming concepts and digital citizenship.

BootUp: https://bootuppd.org/curriculum/
BootUp's curriculum includes projects and resources designed specifically for elementary coders and coding educators with little or no coding experience.

Tynker: https://www.tynker.com/school/courses/show?id=80-programming-300
In this course, students get started with visual block coding, then move on to solving text-based coding problems in JavaScript and Python. Each lesson is designed for a class period of 45-60 minutes. Students learn on their own as they progress through interactive tutorials and coding puzzles, following along to build their own projects. In the first three lessons, students solve puzzles to learn the basics, build a 2-player game using the Tynker physics engine, and apply their coding knowledge to STEM subject areas. In the final two lessons, they move on to text coding in JavaScript and Python.

In section 5, you'll find a detailed description of Bob Irving's dynamic middle school program.

High School

Microsoft Micro-bit curriculum
https://makecode.microbit.org/courses/ucp-science   The **Science Experiments** lessons are geared for students in early high school grades. The lessons are designed help the student gain a greater understanding of the forces and behavior of the physical world. This

is done using methods of observation, measurement, and data analysis. By incorporating the Micro:bit in the experiments, the lessons are a great way to teach both science and computing in the same activity.

AP Principles

Currently, there are two CS offerings through College Board (A)dvanced (P)lacement. The first is called AP Principles and is meant to be a true introduction to Computer Science for beginners. It embraces the project-based mentality, but also infuses some theoretical and "backbone" ideas important in Computer Science. There is much more than just coding in this class. It culminates with a portfolio project that students submit for credit and a test. This class could be offered as early as the 9th grade. The AP Principles program is extremely flexible in that that there are several pre-written curricula that include PowerPoint, worksheets, assignments, tests, lesson notes, project descriptions, and syllabus that can be used--all free of charge. It does not require a Computer Science background to teach this, as long as the teacher is interested in technology and willing to learn. The reception from the community has been incredible--it seems to be reaching incredibly large numbers of students. The feedback from teachers has also been incredible. If you are looking for a place to start, this might be it! There is some programming included in the curriculum but it is more of a survey course based around seven principles called "Big Ideas", and so might be taught be someone who is not necessarily an expert in CS. These ideas are:

Abstraction, Algorithms, Creativity, Data, Internet, Programming

There are several approved syllabi for reference available to anyone (https://apcentral.collegeboard.org/courses/ap-computer-science-principles/course)

Additionally, there are already at least nine approved curriculum providers that also offer a complete curriculum package (free of charge). This number should increase over the next few years.
https://en.wikipedia.org/wiki/AP_Computer_Science_Principles

CS Principles: Code.org https://studio.code.org/courses/csp
The course introduces students to the foundational concepts of computer science and challenges them to explore how computing and technology can impact the world. The AP Program designed AP Computer Science Principles with the goal of creating leaders in computer science fields and attracting and engaging those who are traditionally underrepresented with essential computing tools and multidisciplinary opportunities.

Harvard CS50(H):
https://docs.cs50.net/2016/ap/resources/teaching/teaching.html
CS50 is Harvard University's introduction to the intellectual enterprises of computer science and the art of programming for students with a diversity of technological background and experience.

Beauty and Joy of Computing : http://bjc.edc.org/
In this course, you will *create* apps and other programs using the Snap programming language, you will learn some of the most *powerful ideas* of computer science, you will be *creative*, and you will discuss the social implications of computing, thinking deeply about how *you* can be personally active in promoting the benefits and reducing the possible harms.

Edhesive CS Principles:
https://edhesive.com/courses/apcs_principles
This is an actual class that students enroll in that starts at the beginning of the school year and runs the duration of the academic year. It is perfect for the inexperienced teacher who is not strong in Computer Science skills. It is a complete, full-year course developed in partnership with the University of Texas at Austin's UTeach Institute that focuses on the 7 "Big Ideas" in computer science using

project-based approaches. The course introduces students to the creative aspects of programming, abstractions, algorithms, large data sets, the Internet, cybersecurity, and how computing impacts our world. Students will develop the computational thinking skills needed to fully exploit the power of digital technology and help build a strong foundation in core programming and problem-solving.

MakeSchool AP Principles using SWIFT for iOS

https://www.makeschool.com/online-courses/swift-computer-science-principles

Swift CSP is a free curriculum framework for teachers with a strong focus on Project-Based Learning. This course utilizes Apple's new programming language, Swift, along with interactive playground environments to help students grasp the fundamentals of programming. By the end of the course, students will have built and shipped their own iPhone app.

AP CS

The second AP offering is called AP CS – A. This is the more traditional programming class which has been around for decades and is designed to be similar to a first semester college programming course. It does require the teacher to have some experienced in programming. Currently, it uses the JAVA language and is a blend of theory and Object Oriented Programming (O.O.P) concepts. The class could be taught as a first year course (as many do), but some teachers find that a "primer" course before this is incredibly beneficial. That primer course would not necessarily need to be in JAVA, but would need to introduce students to introductory level programming. The AP test itself is administered on paper, so using paper examinations needs to be part of the experience. It is also important to incorporate the AP vocabulary into the class. College Board has a certain style of question and skill demonstration expectations that students will want to be experienced with. There is no project portfolio expectation for this class or on the test.

There are several textbooks that can be used to guide your AP CS-A classes: https://cb.collegeboard.org/ap-course-audit/courses/computer_science_textbook_list.html

Barbara Ericson has spent years developing a free on-line Java textbook specifically for the AP. It is not only an outstanding command and concept reference, but also an excellent Exam Prep guide with numerous practice questions (multiple choice and short answer) with solutions. A highly recommended resource: https://runestone.academy/runestone/static/JavaReview/index.html

Collegeboard provides a sample syllabus that could be used for an AP CS-A class: http://media.collegeboard.com/digitalServices/pdf/ap/ap-course-audit/ap-computer-science-syllabus-1-id-1172785v1.pdf

Doing well on the final AP tests *should not be the only goal.* Keep in mind not all your students who take the course are taking it because of the test or to get credit in college. Many of the students who take the course just enjoy the topic and want to challenge themselves. They may be looking to expand their academic profile, so getting the five on the test may not be their main motivation. Have those conversations "with your kids, so you know how you design and teach your class. To help prepare, you may have them do practice AP test questions as a regular part of your class. The test itself is about 50% multiple-choice questions and then 50% short answer programming and design questions. College Board makes the current year's short answers questions available in the summer after the test. You should be able to find the last several years' worth of questions out there. There are also several study guides (Pearson, Barrons) that are excellent references and include several sample tests.

Note: The experience of CS at the high school level, even at the AP level, is dramatically different than the experience at the college level. I DO NOT recommend that your students going into CS at the college level skip over that first year class, even if they get an excellent score on the AP test. Each college does CS differently, even using different languages. Faculty at the college level also incorporate elements specific to their own school's vision and their own preference. You want your students to have the full experience of what the college has to offer. So let the motivation for the AP CS class be simply to push students to take a challenging class, NOT necessarily only to do well enough on the test to exempt CS- 101 in college.

Frequently, I hear new teachers ask about how to make decisions about whether to do something in a class based on whether or not it is "on the test." If you have done your research and you still feel like it needs to be part of your class, then it should be. So take the time to answer the unexpected question or watch the newscast about a current event or spend a day exploring a new technology. If you have a thoughtful and dynamic program, it is very likely that students will be plenty prepared to do well on those tests, but if that is the sole focus of your class-- you'll find most of your students will end their Computer Science pathway soon after the AP exam. That is exactly opposite of what we need. Keep your mind open to not letting standardized testing and standards dictate the motivations and flow of your program. Those elements should *support* what you do, not *drive* what you do.

Off-the-shelf curriculum

There are some excellent options here for those who want to use tried and tested curriculum. These options can be both for the beginner teacher or the seasoned veteran. Regardless of who you are, you will still be able to add your own flavor to the class---in fact, it's crucial that you do that! It is what will make your class enjoyable and dynamic, but more importantly your students will connect with it. Following is a description of several online classes/curriculum that can be used to help guide and structure your entire class. They are all well-tested and all provide (free of charge) syllabus, scheduling, handouts, project rubrics, and lesson PowerPoints, quizzes and tests. They can also be used as a resource for you and your students. As a new teacher, they can also be used to help yourself learn the skills and language of the AP curriculum.

Following are several proven curricula used by many teachers across the country, but new programs are approved every year, so this list will be even longer soon. This list is meant to communicate the kinds of options you will have available to you. You will need to experiment to figure out what works best in your program.

CodeHS: AP(H): https://codehs.com/info/curriculum/apjava
This AP Java course is a year-long course designed to help students master the basics of Java and equip them to successfully pass the AP Computer Science A Exam. The entirely web-based curriculum is made up of a series of learning modules that cover the fundamentals of programming. Each module is made up of short video tutorials, example programs, quizzes, programming exercises, challenge problems, and unit tests.

NICERC(National Integrated Cyber Education Research Center)
https://nicerc.org/curricula/computer-science/
According to their website, it is "…a hands-on, projects-based curriculum that utilizes a unique computing platform to engage students in an immersive exploration of the breadth of computer science. Through a puzzle-based learning approach that is strategically meshed with candid discussions of the philosophy and expectations that underlie the learning process, a foundation of problem solving and critical thinking is laid upon which four major

themes of computer science are built. The high-level goals of the curriculum are to (1) Expose students to the beauty of computer science through an engaging discovery process; (2) Show how exploring computer science can be used to solve hard problems; and (3) Cultivate problem solvers who are comfortable at tackling hard problems and who understand that computer science is a lifelong learning process."

CS180@Purdue(H):   https://www.edx.org/course/ap-computer-science-java-programming-purduex-cs180-3x-0
This course is for anyone interested in taking a first-level computer-programming course, particularly those who attend a school that does not provide a similar class.

Java(H): http://programmedlessons.org/java5/index.html
In this computer science course, you will learn the basics of programming in the Java language, and cover topics relevant to the AP Computer Science A course and exam.

There are some excellent paid versions of AP curriculum as well. These are full service programs that include everything you will ever need to teach a class. These would be excellent choices for those new to CS or for teachers less confident in their own CS skills.

A+ Computer Science A:
https://www.apluscompsci.com/material.htm This is an excellent full class-curriculum that includes Lab Assignments (with startup files, descriptions, and solutions), slide shows(with code samples and notes pages), Tests (multiple formats provided including Word, Examview, Moodle, and Blackboard), Quizzes, Worksheets , and solutions and keys.

IMACS: https://www.eimacs.com/educ_apcsoverview.htm This is an excellent full-curriculum with everything you will need for the entire class. It is all on-line and includes everything you need to teach the class, including auto-grading exercises in each section. According to their website, it is *"...Interspersed within a well-organized curriculum are exercises to be completed using an embedded Java compiler, graded coding activities, eight labs, and tests that are graded automatically. Teachers access an "electronic gradebook" to monitor students' progress. The course is designed to be studied either at a student's own pace, or at a pace set by the teacher. This flexibility allows the teacher to permit the more capable students to proceed rapidly at their own pace (and even study the optional, advanced topics), allowing the teacher to more carefully guide the progress of students of lesser ability or motivation."*

Still unsure of where to start?

If you still feel like you are not exactly sure where to start your high school classes, I suggest investigating one of the curriculum listed above for the CS Principles course. It took years to develop, and is one of the best things to happen to Computer Science in recent times, and is *hands-on*. NSF collaborated with College Board and teachers to create a dynamic project-based curriculum for students new to Computer Science. It is extremely well supported with resources and discussion boards for teachers, and there is a huge community around it. It is a common session at many of the technology conferences, especially the CSTA.

Designing your own curriculum

Regardless of what curriculum you use, you'll still need to know about the various skills needed in the curriculum. Especially for the newer AP teacher still building his/her resource library, here is a set of videos that reviews each of the required skills on the AP exam: https://www.youtube.com/playlist?list=PLmpmyPywZ443PFI8YF3ZM moEcRfxXckdH

Once you get a feel for how CS works in the classroom and have a class started, I recommend you create at least one module of class from scratch. What I've found is that when I use another curriculum, I don't have the same motivations, backgrounds, goals, or styles of class as the creators of that curriculum. It does not mean the curriculum is bad or won't work, but it does need your personal touch--and it needs to reach your students. And *you* are the only one who knows how to do that. Designing your own curriculum might sound daunting at first, but once you create that first project that the students really connect with, you will find that is also tremendously vindicating. You will see those light bulbs going off one after another. You will get used to the jumps for joy in the midst of their project, when they finally get it to work, because they spent their own sweat and tears working on it. However, it does take trial and error in the first steps:

....take time to explore!

It will pay off down the road. Teachers out there: try to find the time and energy to explore your own stuff. Change it to fit your style, tweak when appropriate, add what is missing, and remove what does not work. Find some other teachers who are at the same level as you are...*they want to meet you as much as you want to meet them.*

CODE.org has spent a great deal of time and effort to create a series of "inspirational" CS videos for all ages and for all levels. They have taken advantage of a very diverse group of recognizable people to help explain CS concepts as well as inspire students to want to learn more. It's a great resource for both students and teachers: https://code.org/educate/resources/videos

CSFORALL maintains an extensive page overflowing with resources, languages, and other helpful tools for teachers of all levels: https://www.csforall.org/members/

Project and technology ideas:

In this section, I'll describe some technologies and project topics that have worked for us and are common in numerous CS programs across the country.

Web page development:

Website design is always a class favorite. You might get some feedback from hard-core CS guru folks insisting that web design is NOT Computer Science programming. Let me assure you it an awesome tool that works in the classroom! It is an excellent way to let your students see the relationship between text-based commands and actual output on the screen—yet another way to take ideas in your head and bring them to life on a screen. Students can make websites about pretty much any topic. They can redesign an actual existing site; they can create a site for a local business; they can create a site for their club soccer team; or create a site to promote something they care about. A truly interactive site will use HTM5 and CSS, and if you add a backend database to store user entered data from a form, you can use PHP and MySQL. Students can make sites just on their own computer, but if you want to access them online, you'll need to put them somewhere people can get to. We actually purchased a website specifically for this, which also gave the students the experience of uploading their code to a hosting site.

> Note: There are numerous freebie websites which allow hosting (i.e. squarespace.com or WIX), but these are *template-based*, which means you just upload your images and text, and it builds and codes the site *for you.* Not very useful for teaching web coding on the backend.

There are tons of resources, tutorials, and help sites all over the internet for web design, since it has been around for many years. The one that I find is the most useful is w3schools.com. The site is full of code samples and examples. What is great about website projects is that students can make them as simple or as complex and advanced as they like. If you want to make the website truly interactive, you could also explore the language of JavaScript, which would allow you to code things like a shopping cart. Websites work well for middle and high school ages.

For younger kids, you can also use Web Lab from Code.org: https://code.org/weblab

Case Study #1: Web Design Project

(Here is a deep dive into what I do with web design)

(If you are not interested in a deep dive case study, skip this)

Technology: HTML, CSS, MySQL, PHP

This section of class lasts about five to eight weeks. We spend several days exploring webpage design code, introducing the resources, (especially w3schools.com), and exploring live websites. I'll have student each pick a website they that love and one they hate and then present each to the class and why? It's interesting what they focus on. W3schools has "Try it Now" mode which lets us explore CSS and HTML in class quickly. I actually use that as our playground until we start the project. I'll give them a mini-challenge just to make sure they have enough fundamental skills to start the project. Remember, the project is designed for them to LEARN the code through the project, so when they start, they won't actually have all the skills nor know how they are going to do the project. Then we spend a couple days proposing projects. As with all my projects, they have to convince me why their topic and project idea make sense for them. Having a real connection of some type is crucial. Once project proposals are accepted. I give the students a starter folder with a several blank web pages, resource links, and cheat sheets so they have everything they need in one location. Here is the "umbrella" topic from which students can choose.

- Choose an important topic you are passionate about and create a site to bring attention to this area
- Choose a website that tries to convince/persuade the audience about a significant & important issue in the world
- Build a website which compares and contrasts opposing ideas
- Remake a website that already exists on the internet
- Create an actual website for a real organization
- Build a website that teaches how to a something
- Build a retail website to sell a product you are passionate about
- Build website to bring attention to something local that is important to you

There are weekly (graded) check-ins throughout the project to keep them on track and making progress. I like to alternate between "quantity" and "quality" meaning some weeks I just need certain elements to exist, but does not need to look beautiful; then the next check-in would be concerned with look as well as functionality. For example, the first check-in might be a "skeleton" framework meaning all pages physically are created, are named correctly, and there is basic navigation to move between pages. A second check-in would have an interactive navigation with the home page and real content. A third check-in might include the footer and header, plus an RSS feed. The next check-in might be a form for collecting appropriate user input data. I like to spend a couple days talking about databases so they can see how the front-end form can actually save data into an SQL database. I have a few mini-assignments to help them see how databases are design, how data is stored, and how it is retrieved. We actually spend one class working through some examples together to show them the relationship between the webpage and the backend database. Database is actually a *huge* topic; we just skim the surface to give them an exploratory taste. The next check-in will have each student actually creating a single table in a database and then figuring out how to get the form data (name, email address, etc.) into the database. Student learn about embedded code and web API, have to include an embedded Google Map in their website.

What does a typical day look like? The first few minutes is spent reminding students about upcoming assignments, responding to questions about the assignment, sharing student projects, or demonstrating new skills. Students then spend each day working on their projects. Students collaborate as needed. As teacher, I spend my time helping students think about challenges, try to figure out code errors, and guide projects forward. On some days, students type lots of code; other days are spent more high level conceptual with drawing charts or ideas on a whiteboard; while other days are pure research and exploration. Homework assignments include analyzing live websites, comparing webhosting hosting plans, doing a "live" TCP-IP packet-switching simulation during class using a cut-up email message that finds its way through the network of students, researching publicly available JavaScript scripts, and even a "cool CSS" assignment where students find a really cool CSS trick to show class. In every section of class, I like to have at least one assignment related to a current events article (usually from the newspaper or recent magazine) dealing with the current technology, topic, or project. Additionally, I have students research real job boards for web-related opportunities, just to get a feel for the types of jobs, salaries, skills needed, and experience needed. I'll invite a speaker from the industry talk about professional web design, either in person, field trip, or via Skype. Examples are professional web designers and web design company owners. About half-way through the project, we do the "dude, your website rocks" assignment where each student critiques three other assignment, identifying at least two positive items and two suggestions. This allows them to see what others are doing and get new ideas, but also get used to giving and getting feedback.

I actually purchased a real website to host student projects on, so students can see them live. Sites like this only cost $10-$20 per month and the process to upload files to it is a skill I want them to have as well. The project is graded in two ways. One is focused on the "business" side of the project where the focus is on meeting needs of target audience, eye appeal, interactive interface, and high level design. The second rubric is focused on the "required elements" of the project. That is how you can specify the complexity level, skill and command requirements, and components all students need in their project.

Project Description and Proposal document:

In your project proposal, include

1. Describe the type of project you are going to be working on (from choices 1-8 above)
2. Why choose this project? Why/How are you qualified?
3. Describe your specific idea in as much detail as you can. Include any ideas for imagery, color, layout, content.
4. Include a rough draft layout design for each page.
5. Who is your target audience? What will you do to address that audience
6. Why would people visit your site?
7. What will people accomplish on your site? What are the "results" of visiting your site.
8. Is there a site that exists already online doing the same thing? How will yours be different?

Rubric 1: Real World

(100 points)

- **40%** The message of the website is clear. It is clear what the product/site is, does, and who it is targeted towards. Site is appropriate for that audience. Site has real value, purpose, potential in the world. Product, idea, or learning is described in lots of detail. User input appropriate and professional.

- **40%** Layout & Design & Navigation: appropriate, thoughtful and well planned, attractive, creative, logical, symmetric when needed, and works effectively and correctly. Everything is in the right place relative to the page and the site. Layout creative and engaging, yet logical. Colors make sense and are pleasing to the eye. Things that should be lined up ARE lined up. Style of font. Efforts in design to address a specific target population. Pleasing to the eye.

- **10%** spelling, grammar, layout imperfections, small nit-picky mistakes

- **10%** Extra awesomeness. Something unique that is not already in the rubric. A command or skill that you figured out on your own.

Rubric 2: Project Requirements

3 pages

- *Home page(index) with footer area*
- *About Us*
- *Sign Up, Order-Now, Send info*

Navigation Bar

- *Works on all pages. Same/similar navigation on each page*
- *Current page communicated in navigation*
- *placed appropriate, choices make sense in context*
- *creative, interactive, and clear communication*
- *blends well with color scheme*

Homepage:

- *Social Media icons bar*
- *Logo, Company name*

ContactUs/AboutUs

- *Address, email, social media contact info*
- *Who we are, why we are , what we do*
- *Embedded google maps with your address pinned*

Forms

- *Lined up, in logical order, and looks professional*
- *Data collected: relevant, appropriate, and sufficient*
- *CAPTIA security*
- *form has at least 3 different types of INPUT statements(checkbox, textbox, radio button, textarea, pulldown menu, upload, select, data list)*
- *Thank you page appropriately confirms submission and provides link back*

PHP/ SQL Database

- *Submit: Data is collected, transferred to PHP and handed off to SQL without error.*
- *Database table, fields created appropriately & correctly*
- *Admin page: Your admin page should be able to list all current records.*

Anywhere in project
- *Embedded video*
- *Responsive: site must resize with window size*

App Development:

Developing apps is one of the most real things that students can do because it is something they can easily relate to. They use apps all day long so the idea of making their own makes this kind of project a class favorite. One option is block-based programming. In games design, block-based programming tends to be for the younger kids; however, in app design, it is actually really helpful and works well all the way up to high school. I'll challenge you to let students create real apps, not games.

For beginner students, there is an option worth checking out from CODE.ORG called *App Lab*. While at first it seems made for younger kids, it actually gets pretty advanced and even allows text-based code—even in middle and high school. The apps are still relatively simple, but it is a possible stepping-stone between simple block-based and harder text-based code. There are lots of tutorials and resources. code.org/educate/applab .

App Inventor and Thunkable are app design tools targeting middle and high school ages. Android and iOS apps can be made using both environments. Both are easy to use and have lots of tutorials and resources. Students can use an onscreen emulator in place of an actual tablet or phone, although it is not nearly as engaging as an actual phone/tablet. For full effect, I highly recommend getting actual phones or tablets.

For more advanced level of iPhone & iPad apps, students can use X-code software (free, but works *only* on a MAC) to program using the language of **SWIFT**. There is a steep learning curve and takes a while to figure out, but once students see how it works, they can start to do some amazing things. For about $100, students can register to actually submit their app to the Apple App store. There is an iOS-Swift curriculum available by Maker School that you could use for this: (https://www.makeschool.com/online-courses/swift-computer-science-principles)

For more advanced level of Android app design, students can use **Android Studio** (developer.android.com/studio). While this is a powerful tool for app development, it is a professional grade IDE, so it is going to be for your upper level and advanced students. For about $99, students can register to actually submit their app to the Google Play app store.

CodeHS also sponsors a mobile app development curriculum for iPhone and Android. They also have numerous other excellent curriculum available for this level.
https://codehs.com/info/features/mobile_apps

Case Study #2: App Design:

(Here is a deep dive into what I do with app design)

(If you are not interested in another case study, skip this)

Technology: *Android tablets and AppInventor*

This section of class lasts about three weeks. We spend the first few days building some simple apps together that use the basic functionality of the mobile device. I have a project that I love to use because it's based on a true story and also is a great beginner level app that also shows real world value. Some restaurant/bar bouncer from NY(and of course I say it is with a "NY" accent) needed a counter system for keeping track of people going in and out of the business. The fire marshal had been several times and cited them for violations. So he wrote an app with a couple buttons on the screen for IN/OUT. It kept a running count(called a variable) of total people and displayed that on the screen. When he exceeded the limit, the app makes an alert sound and blinks red. Kids love the story and we then create that app together. I want them to understand the difference between writing code for a computer and writing code for a mobile device. We look at how to use button, text boxes, images, camera, accelerometer, clock, sliders, touchscreen, audio and video. I make sure that each day I leave some time for them to explore on their own with the skills they have just learned. After a few days of exploration, students start to research ideas for their project proposal.

For this project, they will design an app that addresses the needs of people with a physical limitation, emotional or learning disorder, psychological disability, mental disability, or other handicap. I like to introduce the section with a video that shows two families whose lives were changed in powerful ways because of apps written to help their children. It is the kind of video you can't help but tear up. I am always amazed at how many students have connections with this population, so they usually respond well to this topic idea. I still give them some freedom to pick their topic. Homework and class work will also include downloading/critiquing real apps on a real tablet, comparing desktop OS programming vs mobile app development, and a review of mobile app languages and development tools. In every section of class, I like to have at least one assignment related to a current events article (usually from the newspaper or recent magazine) dealing with the current technology, topic, or project. Additionally, I have students research real job boards for app developing opportunities, just to get a feel for the types of jobs, salaries, skills needed, and experience needed. After their project gets off the ground, one of their assignments is to research the market for products that are similar to theirs. Then they can do a SWOT analysis of their own project. About half-way through the project, we do the "dude, your app rocks" assignment where each student critiques three other assignments, identifying at least two positive items and two suggestions. This allows them to see what others are doing and get new ideas, but also get used to giving and getting feedback. Our discussion questions deal with videos that deal with real people being helped by an actual app. We'll research careers in mobile app design and study how companies use apps to further their message or enhance their business. Evaluation for this section includes completing three online tutorials, plus submission of a completed app according to the rubric. After students complete that required app, they are allowed to pick an app of their own choosing and spend a week on it. It is evaluated using the same rubric.

Rubric: Required App

15% Addresses a real need in a real way that helps a real person.
20% Uses features, A-list functions, tools of mobile device to address problem. Uses them effectively and takes advantage of what is available on the tablet,
10% Uses B-list components to enhance their project. Uses them effectively
30% Actual "result" is useful, practical, works, and actually does what it is supposed to
20% Appearance is appropriate and professional
5% Creative App Title and Icon. Uploaded to tablet for testing

** A-List and B-list components are listed are on the whiteboard. B-list items require more challenging code and are harder to figure out, but allow for more complex and interactive apps.

Game Design

Game Design is an excellent choice for any grade level and also for any skill level. Many of the concepts and "theory" of Computer Science and programming are actually implemented in most games. I can think of an example in a game for almost any programming command, even very advanced. The energy around games, as most teachers know, is amazing. You can harness that energy. Ask any teacher who teaches games design in the CS classroom. You can have students create games around any topic (i.e. academic subjects, social, serious world problems). There are simple block-based programs, beginner 3D worlds, and then you also have professional level languages that can be used to program games at an advanced level. I'll challenge you to use your game design sections to let students create games that have purpose and value. My advice here is GET OUT OF THE WAY. Too many guidelines, restrictions, rules, and requirements squashes the creativity.

Here are some category ideas for game design:

Serious Games: problems in the world around them
Social Cause: issues in the world that need attention
Educational: helping to learn or teach something
Simulations: business, animal behavior, vehicle
Training: Flight simulator, medical, driving
Board Games: convert any board game

Case Study #3: Game Design

(Here is a deep dive into what I do with game programming)

(If you are not interested in another case study, skip this)

Technology: Python & Pygame

This section of class lasts about eight weeks. We spend the first few days experimenting with game-building components such as adding images, sounds, text, variables, movement, and interaction. The goal is not to teach them those skills but to give them a feel for the programming environment. They will actually develop the skills themselves through the project. By the end, most students write an average of four hundred lines of code to implement a game that addresses a real world social causes or issues such as poverty, disease, depression, natural disaster, political corruption, LGBT community challenges, or animal abuse. I make sure students are aware of the many resources available to them, including thirty+ self-help videos made by me, plus about fifty pages of code samples related to the projects they are doing. Additionally, they can choose to take part of the Star Board, where students can mark a star by a peer's name any time they get help. Very quickly, students love to get stars by their name, so offering help becomes something they love! BTW: There are no rewards of any kind for getting stars. I am looking at the board right now as I write…there are over two hundred starts up there, which means two hundred times students got help in their projects from a fellow student. Awesome.

The weekly discussion questions for this section deal with games being used in non-traditional ways to teach and to solve real problems. Students will research the game industry jobs and careers to see what backgrounds, skills, and salary ranges exist. In every section of class, I like to have at least one assignment related to a current events article (usually from the newspaper or recent magazine) dealing with the current technology, topic, or project. To keep students on task and making continuous progress, there are weekly check-ins. These rotate between quantity (to move them along towards completed project using a checklist style of requirements) and quality (ensuring requirements not only exist, but are done in high quality). For example:

Check-in 1, Level One background, main character, and scoring on screen

Check-in 2: Title Screen complete, Level One almost complete
Check-in 3 Level One complete, Level Two started.
Check-in 4: Level Two complete, Level Three started.
Check-in 5: Level Three complete
Check-in 6: Projects Due

A new level cannot just be a repeat of the previous level. Each new level must have one additional object, one additional challenge, increased complexity, and a new background. Level three will be a culminating "boss" level. I have found that designing regular and frequent check-ins like this, with requirements based on levels, ends up "making" the kids learn a variety of skills by taking advantage of the fact that they want to make a good game and guiding them through the process. It also keeps them on track for the project long-term, but also focused and on-task each day. I rarely find a student not willing to put in extra effort to get their level exactly as they imagine.

What does a typical day look like: After announcing any upcoming assignments or upcoming deadlines, I like to show one or two student projects on the projector for others to see. In some projects, students can "apply" to partner for a project. When I accept those, I always demand that they submit twice the project size and quality. In most cases it pays off allowing that collaboration. Two girls who were very passionate about their medical tool and body system "game" had spent hours out of class working on their navigation and were so proud. They showed the class what they had so far; it was a chance for other students to see another way of approaching a project, but also what good work and progress looked like. It was just for a couple minutes. Then students go into game programming mode. As teacher, I wander around the room helping those in need. Early on, there are lots of questions, but as they become more self-sufficient, they are able to work through many challenges on their own, especially with the help of the resources I provide.

For homework, they will research actual jobs in the industry, see how professional games are made; read several articles and news clips about games being used for social good in the world; test their wits finding as many errors as possible in an error-ridden printout of a badly typed game, critique each other's games and give written feedback, and write a short story from the point of view of the main character of the game giving the backstory for their project. They'll also critique actual educational games and even enjoy a Skype visit from an actual games designer. One of my favorite assignments is their "Deep Dive" assignment where they select a section of code they are really proud of and they explain exactly what it does and how it does it. They can type it, audio record, or video record their deep dive. Being able to explain something technical is something I feel strongly about. As part of their final submission, they'll include a video recording of the game being played, a home page on the "app store" for their game, and a self-graded rubric reflecting what they felt they earned on the project.

After all the games are submitted, we have an end-of-project party where students bring in snacks and we play each other's games for an entire period. What a great chance to celebrate learning and accomplishment.

Self-help video support: I mentioned before that we created numerous self-help videos for each section of class. Here is a sample listing for this section of class for beginning game design:

General Understanding	Random numbers
Inserting images	Winning and losing
Displaying text	Making images disappear
Score keeping	Changing speeds
Keyboard movement	Boolean variables
Mouse movement	Missile firing
Using timers	Changing levels
Counting things	Images collision
Sound effects	Automatic movement
Background music	Understanding variables

Changing levels	Chasing and evading
Boundaries	Arrays of objects
	Dragging something

I mentioned before about the importance of the proposal. Here is a sample of how we invite proposals:

Proposal and topic choice

To introduce this project, I love to show a video made by a high school boy who is complaining about 1st world problems, such as his phone battery life, not enough milk for cereal, or being woken up by the neighbor mowing grass. The students quickly get the point. We talk about first world problems to bring context to the type of more serious world issues we are going to address in our games. I ask them to think about something that matters to them and that is a significant issue in the world. I even provide a list of dozens of possible topics to get them thinking in the right direction. Students are always invited to submit ideas not on the list. After choosing a topic, they "claim" that topic by completing a two-three slide presentation including:

- Why choose this topic? Explain your connection.
- Include one symbolic image that of the topic.
- Include at least one statistic related to the topic.
- Include two additional things that are shocking, surprising, or interesting about this topic.

Project Description and Rubric
Students can earn 90% of points by completing project according to rubric. For those striving for the additional 10 points, there are options at the end

NOTE
___+10 The game plays without errors or crashing

___+10 World issue/game topic Value:

    7.5 Does your game promote, introduce, or teach about the topic/issue you chose?

    2.5 Did you refer to your interesting statistic or fact during game play

___+10 Title Screen and Directions

    2.5 Is there a clever, eye catching, & appropriate title/intro screen with your name on screen clearly visible?

    2.5 Does the intro screen(s) display an introduction storyline?

    2.5 Are there directions & objectives ?

    2.5 Pleasing to the eye

___+10 Game Images Are there appropriate & high quality graphics/images?

    ___+20(10 each level)

    5 At least 1 additional/new object on each level 2 and 3

    5 At least 1 significant change in complexity & difficulty in each level 2 and 3?

___+15 Game Play & Mechanics

    5 Did you handle all movement, boundaries, edges, collisions.

    5 Is there at least one sound effect (or background music) that enhances game play as well as makes sense in context?

    5 "how to play," "how to control," "how to succeed," "what to do" is easy to pick up and is communicated

___+10 Scoring & feedback System:

    5 Is feedback/scoring prominently and clearly displayed on screen

    5 Does it calculate appropriately & logically and make sense in the context of your game topic?

___+5 End Game

    Can you win and lose? Does it display correctly? Does it make sense in context?

    Can you go back and play again (for entire game or on any one level)

Additional Points: Choose your BEST +10 points

__Add an addition 4th level (+10)

__Animation (+5)
__A second scoring system (+5)
__"Menu" that lets you see directions, see story, and/or play (+5)
__Record your own sound or music (+3)
__Your own image in the game and it makes sense why (+3)
__1000 lines or more of functioning code (+5)
__ timer (+3)
__Boolean True and False variables (+3)
__Random number usage (+3)
__Missile firing or similar (+5)
__Dragging objects (+3)
__HELP screen implemented (+3)
__Work, complexity, skills, and effort and accomplishment FAR beyond expectations in level 1,2,3 (approved by teacher only)(+?)

Robotics:

Earlier in the book, we identified several robots that can be incredibly effective learning tools in the Computer Science classroom. You'll find that robotics tends to be attractive to both boys and girls. Bots are incredibly hands-on and out–of-your-seat kinds of technologies. Wait until you see the energy and sense of accomplishment on their faces when their robot does exactly what they tell it. You can read about our middle school robotics module in the resources section at the end of the book. What robots offer is a way for students to actually program something to interact with the environment. They can detect heat, light, sound, pressure, color, and even motion. Most robots have motors, lights, arms, wheels, pulleys, levers, trays, or even legs that can be programmed to move in reaction to the environment around. It's one of the most engaging and interactive experiences you can have with technology. I recommend this as one of the first risks you take…kids love it! (teachers, too) You can set up obstacle courses, challenge courses, races, multi-bot challenges, navigation scenarios, times challenges, even sumo events.

Case Study #4: Autonomous cars & robots

(Here is a deep dive into what I do with robotics)

(If you are not interested in another deep dive case study, skip this)

Technology: *Thymio Robots*

This section of class lasts about three weeks. After two days of introducing movement, sensors readings, colors and sounds, I throw them into their projects. This section of class is a bit different from the other sections that I do. Over the years, I have explored many variations and the current strategy is my favorite. Over the course of a few weeks, students are working both independently and collaboratively to complete the car challenges. When they think they have done it correctly, they demonstrate it to me. What that looks like is students running to me, "Mr. Bergman, I got it. Watch this. Do I get a check?" "Hmmm. Well, it did not quite do what the assignment says. Go make and make a couple adjustments and try again." They run back, type some code, retest, and eventually get it working and then come running back. Pure chaos, but amazingly the common thread is engaged students all working on a series of projects, solving them in whatever ways they can, excited to be learning and making progress. In end-of-class evaluations, it is always listed as one of the favorite sections of class. It is extremely out-of-your-seat. I ask them to bring the "sign off" sheets to me each time. This makes for easy grading and progression tracking. Students complete a series of self-driving car related projects that mimic what the new driverless cars would have built in to their circuitry: "crash avoidance," "car passing," "avoid potholes," "crazy parking lot," "Parallel parking," "parking garage," "overheating," "pedestrian voice activation," and "accident detection". The last project is called Robot Art, where student choice and creativity come out. Some students will spend days on this going through numerous sheets of paper. They produce a 2'x3' "drawing" on which 100% of the writing and drawing on it is accomplished by the robot itself through code. These go up on my walls. Students who finish early can attempt advanced challenges such as an obstacles course timed race between two people or try to program the robot to balance itself on top of a big red ball. Discussions during this section include watching/reflecting on videos of robots in various industries, Ethical Dilemmas (students can  test their courage attempting the moralmachine.mit.edu) in decision-making for driverless cars, ethical considerations for humanoid robots; we watch the first part of Disney's movie A.I. to talk about emotions in robots, we watch parts of Bicentennial Man to talk about humans becoming robotic and vice versa. Evaluation for this section of class is based on completion of the required car challenges. We read Runaround from Isaac Asimov where he introduces the three laws of robotics. Students actually spend time in a class CHAT room talking about the short story.

Project Description and Rubric

____ Intro Challenge (20 points)
Move straight ahead 3 seconds, spin counter-clockwise for 3 seconds, backup 4 seconds, turn 90 degrees left, straight for 2 seconds, spin clockwise 5 seconds. Make the top LED light BLUE, then make a complete triangle approximate 1 foot per side, then make a complete circle approximately 2 feet in diameter. Make any alarm sound. Turn all CIRCLE lights ON. Top light OFF. Robot STOPS.

2. Autonomous CARS Missions (10 pts each)
___**Crash Avoidance:** If another car approaches closely from directly in front or behind, turns sharply and moves AWAY from the oncoming vehicle FAST

___**Pot Hole:** In the event there is a major pothole or sink hole, or major road drop, we need to have the car detect that so it does not drive into the hole. Your autonomous car should be able to drive in any direction and if it finds an EDGE (i.e. desk edge), it backs up, makes a turn and continues in another direction. Car should be able to move around without stopping or falling off for thirty seconds.

___**Pedestrian Screams:** There may be situations where a pedestrian might need to communicate to a moving car to STOP. Your car should continue until a loud YELL is detected, stopping the car immediately

___(partners) **Crazy Parking Lot**: Three cars have to roam around the top of any desk without falling off or hitting another car

___**Accident Reaction:** Car moves forward until something actually hits it (tap, stopping immediately and sounding an alarm

___**Overheating**: Autonomous cars have to monitor all aspects of the vehicle, including temperature inside the vehicle and engine to prevent car overheating. Let's set the TOP lights BLUE to indicate a cool temperature. Find the ceramic heater in the room. If your robotic car detects heat over a "normal" threshold, it should sound an alarm three times to communicate. We'll also turn on all TOP Lights RED. When it hits the half-way point, I want it to turn YELLOW and beep one time

___ (Two partners) **Pass me by** Autonomous cars have to be able to handle human drivers as well. As two cars approach each other head-on in the same lane, each has to get out of way to let the other pass, then get back in lane to continue driving. One of you is the go forward car, one is the car that avoids.

___**Parallel parking**: Autonomous cars need to be able to park autonomously as well; especially downtown, the ability to parallel parking is crucial. Your car will drive forward until we hit one of the buttons, which puts it into parallel parking mode. Use your FRONT and BACK infrared detectors to negotiate a spot which is approximately ½ way between the two. NOTE: the distance between the two cars might be different when you run your code.

___(partner) **Parking Garage**:   Press button to start at the "entrance." You are allowed to "PUSH" and "PULL" your robot-car in order to find a BLACK road. That road will be on a slight incline. Then it should follow that road until it ends. Once at the top, it can use its edge of road logic (pot hole) to find its way to the TARGET parking space. The parking place is right in front of the wall. Park your car there. Turn top colors to GREEN to indicate completion and STOP the motors.

___Art Open Ended: create 100% robot-drawn masterpiece including first or last name initial

Arduino & Raspberry-Pi

Earlier in the technology section, we discussed these as very effective learning tools in the CS classroom. This is one of the most exciting technologies of the last few years because it is so expandable, **and dirt cheap**. It is the DIY gift from heaven. In the same way that code allows us to take ideas in our mind and put them to life on a screen in front us, the Arduino/Raspberry-Pi gives us that same power but as an entire miniature computer system with sensors that can detect almost anything. Tons of resources, books, and tutorials exist for middle and high schoolers. Raspberry-Pi computers are complete mini-computers that need a keyboard, mouse, and monitor. They usually come preinstalled with programming software. There are lots of DIY projects on-line as well as several books on Amazon. Arduino boards are awesome for engineering level projects using sensors. They might be a bit more advanced because they require some hard core coding and wire connections to make them work. Again, there are lots of DIY projects online as well as several books on Amazon.

Under the Hood

This section of class lasts about one to two weeks. If you can find some older desktop and laptop computers, you can let students take them apart and rebuild them. Students love this and learn so much. You will be amazed at how much they will learn in just a few days. But *do not*, I repeat, **DO NOT** stand in front of them and show them a component, define and describe it, and let them watch you. This has to be done on the floor, in groups of two or three opening up the desktop case with screw drivers, taking out the RAM, hard disk, and video card. You want student touching all the pieces, talking about what they pieces do, any numbers associated with the pieces (size, speed, quantity, etc.), connecting them and inserting them where they are supposed to be. Advanced students will even remove the fan, heat sync, and CPU. You might even add in an old network switch (talk to your IT dept.) and let the kids "plug" into a mock local Ethernet network. Get a collection of old laptops and let the kids open them up, remove anything that can be removed. Give them ads from the Sunday paper to learn hardware vocabulary, speeds and sizes of components, and manufacturer names. Give them "money" to go online and buy replacement parts. Every couple days, have them upgrade the RAM memory of one of the laptops. Take the kids on a field trip to the IT department network/server room. For homework one night, they have to explain the entire boot-up process of the computer to their mom and dad at the dinner table. It never fails, I get numerous emails from parents who are soooooo impressed with their daughter understanding and explanation--then they usually ask me how to fix something on their computer.

Case Study #5: Hardware: Under the Hood

(Here is a deep dive into what I do with hardware)

(If you are not interested in another case study, skip this)

Technology: motherboard, RAM, hard-drive, video card, CPU, power supply, old laptops, old switches, network cables

Students will put together and take apart laptop and desktop computers. They will also "purchase" replacement parts online and learn to update and upgrade computers. Over the course of several classes, we'll go through exactly how a computer works at the hardware level. They'll will be familiar with all the vocabulary as well as the specifications of a computer. They will take apart and rebuild both a desktop and laptop computer several times during this section. I have a collection of four or five mini-projects that students work on in- between building computers. Those assignments require students to go online to find the specs of two really good laptops and do a head-to-head comparison. I also have them compare the hardware specs of the current top mobile phones. They actually create a crossword puzzle using all the words from the hardware section. The hard (and best) part is coming up with the clues. They will exchange puzzles and students who can complete it without help can get a bonus point. Another assignment includes a description of several "tech problems" that are hardware, related and they have to identify what the problem is and offer a solution. We take a short "field trip" down to the server network room where students can see behind the scenes and also ask questions of our IT director. Every other day,1/2 the class will sit in a big circle with a huge pile of hardware components; we pass them all-around and talk about how it all fits together to make a working computer. Over the course of a couple weeks, the numbers, speeds, sizes, and dimensions start to make sense to them. Why a USB thumb drive is thirty-two GB instead of twenty-two GB actually makes sense. If there is time, we will even spend a day converting binary numbers into letters and numbers, and once they figure out how to do it, we actually code a message to send to the Mars Rover, asking it to rotate the camera seventeen degrees and take a photo with the shutter open ten seconds.

I actually do a hands-on interactive quiz in this section. This would include doing actual hardware component upgrades including identifying RAM memory, installing a second hard-disk, and replacing a video card from a collection of parts. They will be given several hardware-related problem scenario descriptions that and describe how they would troubleshoot. They have to describe the differences in the specifications of a high-end and low-end computer.

The section culminates with two big projects: Students have to build a computer (and describe the parts while doing it) while blindfolded and they have to outfit an entire small business with all technology with only a modest $3K budget.

Here is the sample of the small business project description

You've just graduated from college and were hired in at an excellent salary. Your boss asked you into her office to talk about what would be needed to outfit their new office. She is going to let you prove yourself. giving you authority to spend maximum $3500. You are eager to impress your boss by finding some excellent equipment that meets all their needs, and are able to do that at lower-than-expected total costs. You have heard that she is a no-nonsense business executive; if she feels as if you skimped on quality or did not meet the specifications, especially because this is your first project…she might fire you. If you do go over or under $3500 significantly, explain WHY?

(You may use BestBuy, TigerDirect, Newegg, Amazon, etc)
Part1: New Computers
    1.   For Architect: One high-end Windows or MAC desktop with large monitor: great graphics, powerful CPU, lots of RAM, tons of disk storage
    2.   For Office Assistant: One lower end off-the-shelf laptop
    3.   For Sales agent: tablet style laptop or iPad
Part 2: Extra parts & Upgrades
    1.   NVidia or AMD Video Card, in order to run advanced 3D Design software
    2.   2+ TB external hard disk for backup storage
    3.   1 TB internal hard drive

4.	RAM DDR memory. Need an 8 GB chip upgrade in order to run 3D Design software

Part 3 Network and Printing

1.	Wireless black /white Laser printer
2.	Wireless(Wi-Fi) router for the office

Make a GOOGLE DOC spreadsheet with specific details

What you bought (include maker & model name, i.e. HP 2700)

Details of important key words (i.e. 750 GB Seagate drive)

Where you bought it (URL) (i.e. Walmart.com/)

Price (i.e. $75.87)

Section Three

The project-based approach

In my classroom over the last twenty years, I have noticed my students are more engaged and eager to learn when they have a challenging project to work on, as opposed to working through a textbook chapter by chapter. When students work on self-directed projects, their motivation is to see their idea *come to life*. They are willing to work hard and push further when it is valuable to them. When you go through a textbook, chapter-by-chapter, skill by skill, then the motivation is to get through the chapter, do some questions at the end of the chapter, and have a quiz on Tuesday. "Why are we studying this? Because it's on the test." No. No. and No. Additionally most practices in the chapter are able to be completed in a matter of minutes, perhaps a bit longer for larger assignments. There is not really a chance for the skill to sink in or to connect it with something they can relate to. When you do longer projects (our projects usually last from a couple days to several months), there is time for students to connect with it. They can work through their problems, reap in the joy of their successes, or wallow in the frustrations. You can relax also knowing that it is ok if they struggle during their project---there is time for that struggle to happen. The most effective teachers will tell you that it is **when they struggle with something that the best learning happens**. When the textbook leads the class, that emotion and connection simply does not happen on its own. I am not saying they won't learn anything that way, but I am saying the difference in the engagement factor is night and day. Use your textbook as a reference to help accomplish their projects.

The project-based classroom requires a different way of thinking from students, teachers, parents, and administrators. It requires teachers to surrender some of the control and power normally associated with traditional classrooms. It requires students to be active, pro-active, and in control of their own learning. It requires that teachers and students work side-by-side, finding ways for students to motivate and lead themselves through their own learning progression. This environment and structure requires administrators to have different expectations from their CS faculty. It requires a different definition of success, but also a different definition of failure. It requires a different way to grade and evaluate.

And it takes practice.

I believe the kinds of students who experience this type of class will be engaged with Computer Science in the ways that we need them to be able to solve problems in the world "out there." I believe we need to be producing students who can DO, not just KNOW. I believe we need students who can create and apply, not just regurgitate information. I believe we need students who are comfortable figuring things out on their own rather being handed "correct" answers or memorized solutions. I believe we need students who have developed an ability to express themselves through technology and are not afraid to dive deep into that technology and get their hands dirty.

Once their projects get going--that is where the magic happens. It's where we see the successes, but also the failures. Get ready for mistakes, lots of errors, lots of "going down the wrong road," and lots of answering questions with questions. Those mistakes and errors will be the most valuable components of a project-based program. Anytime they can figure something out on their own--even if it takes longer-- that is always better than hearing it from me. Or better yet--if a fellow student can explain how to do something--even better-- because in the real world that is often how it happens--your classroom can emulate that environment. In the PBL class, just as in life, there is never one answer to a problem. You want your class to embrace that.

Defining projects

The power of using projects in the classroom especially comes to life when you have defined, *thoughtfully,* the parameters of your projects. There is a balance you'll need to find between open-ended/student choice, requirements and guidelines, and skills. You are going to use the project as the tool that the student will use to learn a specific set of skills. This is where your project definition and description come into play. For example, in a game design project if you just say "make a game," then you are going to not get the best from your students. Instead, find an "umbrella" topic that you want all students to fall under. In our game design class (you can read about this in the Game Design Case Study), students are required to choose any issue in the world (such as hunger, disease, natural disaster, nuclear testing, or gender inequality) and create an interactive game-like experience where every image, challenge, sound effect, and score are all related to the chosen topic. The game is just another avenue they can use to communicate their ideas. In our app design section, we ask students to choose an app that helps a person in society with a disability, handicap, or limitation.

In either case, the number one thing I look for in their project proposal is that they connect with the topic. They have to have some real reason why they chose that topic. If they don't connect, they will quickly lose interest. In the project rubric, this is where you design the project so that in order to accomplish all the items on the rubric, they will have to use a specific skillset (or command set) which you have defined (formally or informally) in your learning objectives. This does take some time to master (I am still "perfecting" it even now.) What this allows you to do is get really good at accepting project proposals. Keep sending them back until they convince you about their topic choice, as well as the complexity of their project itself.

Project proposals

I hope it is beginning to be obvious why the proposal is tremendously important in the PBL classroom. In the project-based classroom, you'll find that student choice is incredibly effective for successful projects (it is perhaps the most important aspect.) Design high-level project "umbrella" topics such that students can choose something under that for their project. Help them propose a thoughtful & worthy project. Use a formal project proposal document including reasons why they chose it. Don't let them select something they don't really connect with. I make the proposal a major assignment grade to get their attention and require several items in order for me to accept. Have them research the topic and submit a formal project proposal including topic choice, project description, motivations, interesting statistics, stories, images, video, or facts related to the topic. Those help develop that connection which is crucial. In the proposals, if they don't convince you, make them resubmit. Play that game a bit with them and you'll get better project proposals---and ultimately better projects. It's worth starting a day late to get them to identify a good topic.

Projects to *learn*, not to *demonstrate*

The project-based classroom that I am proposing uses projects *to actually learn the skills*, not just to demonstrate *after* learning. This is a tremendously important idea to grasp because it is opposite of what classrooms tend to do. Students will choose their projects and even start them without knowing yet how they will do them. That is something you (and they) might not be used to. It is a class where students lead their own learning and have genuine choice in the projects they work on. Keep in mind their other classes are not like this; you'll have to prove that you really mean it. We use the project itself as a tool to help students see the need for as well as the skill of actually using a specific concept or command or technology or language. This type of learning environment encourages lots of questions. Be ready for them, but also be ready for how you will respond to them; not every student should get the same response. It all depends on how that student learns best.

> Overheard at the CSTA '17 conference, "...*I am here for the questions, not the answers...*"

Needing and wanting to know how to do something is one avenue towards helping students find motivation to work hard towards their own learning. Note: This is very different than the experience most students will have in other classes, so be flexible, but persistent.

Exploration & Experimentation

The most effective project-based CS teachers talk about the value of exploration as a fundamental aspect of success in Computer Science classroom. As you explore new technologies and languages, build in time just to explore. What this looks like in the classroom is just to make sure to plan a few days while introducing a new technology just to get used to the programming environment, language, and technology. *What I have found in CS is that leading an entire class through a "follow me" style of coding seldom works effectively.* Yes, sometimes it is unavoidable, but in general, the results are seldom what you intended. There is such a large variation of skills among the students. One kid is three steps ahead, one kid is still booting his computer, one girl locked herself out, another laptop does not have license code entered, one new kid deleted the sample code you gave them, etc. But what might work is to repeat that introduction a couple times for those who feel like they want to go through the introduction again. Record a couple Kahn Academy style videos that they can go through at their own speed. Challenge the students who learn quickly to figure out some advanced skills. I find that a one-page document with a bunch of sample code on it is exactly what those advanced students want. In our robotics section, I give them a two-page cheat sheet with code samples for most things they'll want to do. That is usually enough to get them started exploring! Once the project gets started, I still offer students time to explore. I encourage them not to begin the project until they feel comfortable with the things we did in the intro. This is also important because, for many students, the technology you are using might be the first time they have used it or even seen it. You want them to be able to engage with it without the stress of project deadlines, tests, and assignments. That can come later, but not in the early days. The more they connect with it, the better their efforts and accomplishments will be in the projects that follow.

Learning how to help

First, learn how to help students select projects which have relevance and *meaning to them*. That comes along with learning how to design projects descriptions so that student will need to use the content and skills you want them to use. Learn how to ask more questions than give answers. Allow and help students to define their own goals and how they want to be held accountable. Learn how to evaluate projects that are unique. Help students understand that failure is not something to be avoided, but actually encouraged. As my colleague, Bob Irving, has written on the wall in his lab, "Fail fast and fail often." Design a grading system which allows students of various skill levels to succeed in projects. Learn how to develop a classroom that embraces student-student collaboration.

Your role here as a teacher shifts to *an assistant* to the students. Not *of* the students….*to* the students. Don't freak out! This is a good thing if done well. But, yes, you are going to have to learn to give up some "control." Your goal now is to help students accomplish the projects they proposed. You are there to help them take the ideas in their mind, break those down into bite-sized chunks, and learn how to implement those pieces line-by-line in code. This takes some getting used to, because you are going to help each student differently, depending on their own skill level, potential, ambition, effort, and even mood. You can challenge them more or less as needed.

Something that you are going to need to address, which is not obvious is how you implement that system of *class help*. Think about it: if five students have their hands up, and it takes five minutes to help each student, then it is going to be 25 minutes before you get to some of them. They can't just sit there "stuck" doing nothing for that time. Early on in the project, they might feel like they don't know enough to work on their own, but encourage them to work on other elements of the project during that time, help another student, or just watch someone else work to get ideas. You have to remember, the students want to work on their own project, so sitting there doing nothing is not something they want to do. The first thing I always ask them when helping is, "What have you tried already?" If they have made no effort to address their problem, I'll usually ask them to try something first and then I'll come back. They quickly learn that they need to make some effort beforehand---and we teachers know that in many cases, they can solve their own problems—if not—then they are developing a troubleshooting skill. In some of my classes, students have asked me to use a "Five-minute rule" where I can only help a student for max-five minutes, and then I have to move on. In

Page 110

other classes, they have asked me to stay with a student as long as necessary. Other classes have had "priority levels" to help decide who should get help next. In the end, I have not figured out the best choice, because ultimately it depends on the specific student as to what type of help she needs at that specific moment in time and at that point in her project. Sometimes your weaker student just needs a quick "put a colon here" or "drag this block here" hint, while other time they might need an entire conceptual "mini-lecture". **NOTE:** When you do those mini-lectures, always announce it to the rest of the class, and you'll find there are always several others who come to listen. "Hey class, Jenny is working on using the accelerometer to determine if her robot is on an incline. If that is something of use in your project, come on over to the whiteboard."

One of the most crucial elements to project-based learning is self-reliance of the student. If you have a thoughtful and appropriate collection of resources, students can help themselves! Later in the book, I describe my collection of code-snippets and "Kahn Academy" style of videos. Over the course of a year, you can develop a project specific collection of resources the students can use. And because you know the common questions students ask, you can have resources specifically to address those common questions. I have over thirty videos in my 9th grade Python section of class, plus a searchable (but not copy/paste-able) code-snippets document to show examples of various commands being used. Students quickly learn that many of their questions can be answered using those resources, and because those are all online, they can be accessed even out of class. What I especially like about these videos is that it is *me* doing them, so they get my voice and personality, so I can refer to things in the video that I know I also say in class. Every few weeks, I add new videos and new code-snippets. In a project-based class, this type of help is one of the most important things you can do.

The multi-sensory CS classroom

Let them use their cell phones, make and respond to surveys, watch videos, respond to discussions, read articles, BLOG, research cool gadgets, make flipgrid movies, make and do puzzles, explore, discuss, collaborate, make and play games, get out of their seats, explain their code and projects, critique in peer-to-peer reviews, and do lots of presentations. Let students suggest how they would like to be evaluated. Let them post questions in online forums and discussion boards. Let them ask experts in the community to find answers to their questions. Take them on field trips. Create learning experience that lets them engage with the content and energy of your class in ways that you cannot otherwise. Your job as a teacher in the PBL CS classroom is to design a set of projects and a class structure that allows for that type of class engagement. The tools of Computer Science and technology are extremely interactive, responsive, and dynamic. Make sure your class reflects that. *Do Not* let your class be an in-seat, quiet, and passive experience.

The project-based classroom does not happen instantly, but students will start to understand the style of class, the focus on learning and making progress rather than on summative grades, the feeling of ownership of their own learning, and they build the confidence to bring their own ideas to life. It is also your job to get out of the way when needed. Lou Zulli, one of the most recognized and innovative teachers in the U.S. once gave me some "Mark Twain"-inspired advice, ".... don't let school get in the way of good education."

If that sounds like a classroom you'd like to be part of, then you are reading the right book.

CS homework

Ewwwwwwwwwwww. Homework. I really want you to pay attention here. This homework topic is one of the most important conversations that the world of education does NOT have. Kids hate homework and for the most part don't do it. Can you blame them? Most homework is rote, repetitive practice, thoughtlessly given because "my class will have homework every night"—as opposed to an assignment intentionally designed for a specific class because it adds specific value. Think differently, so you don't get lumped into the "Oh God, not homework" pile each night. When your students are not in your classroom, you want them to think about their project and your class. You want your class to be the one Johnny or Suzy talk about at the dinner table. They are going to get an overabundance of *coding* in your class, so don't feel like you need to give them additional coding assignments for homework. If it is important to you, *DO IT IN CLASS*. Use homework as a way to get them to interact with CS in ways you really cannot during class. Use homework as a tool to let them connect CS with the outside world. I usually have one-two assignments per week, each of which requires real thought but are less than ten-fifteen minutes in total time needed. Students are always welcome to work on homework during class time and vice versa. Some successful ideas include:

Online discussions
Students lead classroom online chat
Watch news reports, documentaries
Current CS events
Read CS newspaper articles
Research CS and technology topics
Find cool tech blogs or discussion boards
Review products
Find out about not-yet-on-the-market technologies. Discuss moral, legal, and cultural issues related to those technologies.
Read a short story related to the project technology

Write a short story related to the project technology
Watch a movie that relates to the project technology
Research jobs in project technology related industry
Real World interviews: Have students research a person somewhere in the world to interview.
Find images of CS and technology used in different industries
Find images of current project technologies

Flipped CS Classroom

("flipping" what goes on in-class and out-of-class)

Ahhhhhhhhh. Run for the hills…he used a terribly overused and seldom understood cliché. I don't use a stereotypical flipped classroom, but I do have a bunch of Kahn Academy style of videos for my students that are specifically tailored to the projects that we are working on. In my introductory classes, I can anticipate the common questions or skills they will need in order to complete most projects. So, over the years, I have found a common twenty-five questions that they tend to have, and have made short two-four minute videos all using the same example so they are familiar with it. They can be used as a resource for students for specific concepts and skills. Those are great for kids who need to see the code and hear me talk about as they are watching. Yes, those videos include all my stupid jokes and dog barking in the background. It makes it real for the kids. Additionally, I have a Google Doc (We are a Google school) with fifty+ pages of code samples, keyword searchable, so if they can describe in one or two words what they are trying to do, there is usually a code snippet to show them how to get started. What I love about this style of learning is that because my example is the same in all code samples and videos, I know that they cannot just reuse my code. I make sure that my example is FAR different than theirs. So, they have to convert the code samples into their own project. This gives them the ability to work on projects outside of class, and yet still have access to their teacher. I add, remove, and edit videos for every class every year.

Probably the #1 thing I can recommend to any CS teacher is to provide resources like these for every class.

Failure

Projects are full of failures. Longer projects lead to better failure. WHAT???!! We talk about how failure should be embraced in education, but what does that even mean? Few schools even attempt it. In the CS classroom, students will fail most of the time in the class. In order to get that simple ten-line program to work perfectly, they will get it to NOT work twenty times. Eventually, they get the result they were seeking. He or she who is willing to make mistakes the most frequently makes the most progress. Isn't that the exact opposite of most classes?   In real life, seldom is there only one solution to a problem, so why do we pretend there is during school?   In the CS classroom, there is never one way to do something! What works for one student may not work for another---and that is a great thing. Rarely is there is copy-paste solution in the project-based curriculum. When kids help other kids on their projects, they have to explain so other kids understand and can put it to use in *their own* project. This leads to true and natural collaboration. **Make sure your rubric allows for this environment;** don't say you support failure, yet penalize students on grades any time they make a mistake. Reward progress, effort, commitment, and accomplishment.

I'd like to talk about failure *by the teacher* as well. Computer Science teaching is a journey, not a destination. Sorry for that incredibly cheesy cliché, but it fits perfectly. You are going to try projects that will not go well. You are going to explore a technology which just does not jibe with your students. There will be classes where the project adjustments you make will backfire. Sometimes your rubric will not reflect the grading accurately. Any time you try a new style of project, or technology, it is going to take you a couple times to get it right--that is not a bad thing, but realize that during those early times, there are going to be some kinks--do NOT let your students and their grades pay for the price as you figure things out.

What are some of my failures? Lots. At least as many as my successes.

I have experimented with partnerships with other teachers, schools, businesses that did not pan out. I have taken students on field trips that were not engaging. I tried a new style of culminating event that just did not have the spark I was looking for. I've mistakenly deleted a student's entire project. I've taught languages before I was an "expert." I've began a project only to realize right after that it was the wrong project for this class and this technology. I have had invited speakers into our CS classroom who did not "get" what we were trying to do. I have had Skype calls with industry experts lose connection right in the middle. I have encouraged students to continue to explore an unknown technology, and they never got it to work. I have allowed students to do independent study work, but did not get the expected commitment or accomplishment. I have stretched myself too thin, which resulted in classes and projects falling short. I have purchased bad technology. I have invested in technologies which never made it into my curriculum. I've been asked questions I could not answer. I've been stumped by strange coding errors. Actually, when students get really serious errors-- you know, the kind that crash the entire system--- we actually celebrate and put a screen shot on the wall of fame.

So, yes I have failed. My students have failed. Their projects have failed. And each time we learned what went wrong and tried to do better the next time. One reason why our program has been successful is because in most cases, we did make whatever changes were necessary, researched what was needed, abandoned ineffective ideas, addressed elephants in the room, and went with my gut instincts. My recommendation for you and your students:

> *Expect and embrace failure; it is your best chance to succeed.*

Handling Failure and the Unexpected

It's easy to say "embrace failure" or let your students fail" or that the best learning happens through failure. But what does that actually look like in the classroom? Let's look at some examples: in one of my classes, students were required to create a tutorial video for an entire project, so that someone else could follow the steps to replicate the experience. This video would actually be used by their parents during the student's final exam to try to accomplish the project. On this night, Trey came to me just a few minutes before start time saying that his video file was corrupted and it was his only copy. I had fifteen students there each with their own parents, so had no time or way to be of much assistance. Trey was a good kid, and also a calm student. Instead of freaking out and storming out in panic, he asked if he could do the tutorial *live*. LIVE?!! No way! Woah, that was a huge risk! Things could go really wrong; we had never done this before; we had no idea how the parents would react. Could the students remember all the steps with this added new pressure. How would I grade it? Was it fair to him or the other students? All those considerations as he waited for a response. "Mr. Bergman, please." I said ok. Long story slightly shorter: It was amazing. He loved it. Parents loved it. The could see their boy in action. I was able to see him teaching a challenging set of skills. And I could actually hear his explanations and responses to their questions. I could see him troubleshooting issues and problems as they arose. It was everything

I was looking for in the event. It was right then that I decided that, in the future, all students would teach their parents in person, *LIVE*! Since then it has become one of our most successful events that we do in our department. I could have failed the kid. I could have made him rearrange his schedule, redo the entire tutorial video, and retry at another time. I could have stuck to my guns and rules and it could have ended in a negative way. Instead, what started out as a failure led to an incredible success. Be flexible: both YOU and the students. One of my girls lost her entire project on a Friday that it was due. She had spent weeks programming and it had turned out ok. After school that day, she came in mid-panic and so I asked her to get her backup...she did not have one. The end of the quarter was coming soon, there was not really any time to compromise. I told her the only option I had was to give her until Monday am 8:00am. If she wanted to try to recreate it by then, which would not really be possible. Well, not only did she complete it, it was far better than her original. She said she learned more that weekend than she did in the previous month. She was forced to figure out all the issues, problems, syntax errors, and logic errors on her own...with the pressure of a huge deadline looming. I could have held firm and made her take the hit for an incomplete assignment. Instead she turned an incredibly frustrating and negative event and turned it into one of the most positive experiences of the semester. This actually happened to two girls that semester. In both cases...same result. One of my students asked if he could try a really out-of-the-box project that involved several technologies, none of which he had experience with. I loved the potential in him and the project, so we agreed to explore for a couple weeks. Every day, he experimented with this, with that. It did not work time and time again. Two weeks later, he was still struggling. I told him maybe it was time to give up and try another project. He asked to try for two more weeks. Again. Same thing. And so it went for two months. Now, understand he was making more and more progress each time, learning more and more about the technology, the new language, and a new type of device. Every few days, I would ask him if he was tiring of the challenge, but he always has one more idea to try. I had no idea how I was going to grade this.

It was not failure, but then again it was. He had not accomplished his goal, but he had learned a huge amount of knowledge. The entire class on some days would sit with him to help. One student in particular took a real interest in the project and soon formally joined. Together they learned an entire operating system, a programming language, networking, and tremendous troubleshooting skills. I'll argue what they learned through those several weeks was far beyond what he might have learned had the project come together as he planned. Do those students fail because they did not meet the objectives of their proposal? Absolutely not. In fact, they presenting about their experience in front a set of judges, just as the other students did. The judges were just as impressed with their failure as they were the successes of the other students. A new girl to our school had never really done much with technology, so when we started developing apps, she was far behind the rest of students (who had been taking CS for several years at our school). This girl worked hard in class, came in on breaks and after school. I was there on the due date where she was in lab till 5:00pm working on her app. I remember hearing her scream with excitement because she had gotten a simple button to work as part of her project. Granted, compared to the other students in the class, that working button was something they had working on day one. So, her getting it work on day ten was not so impressive. Or was it? As I sat there sharing her delight looking through her "completed" project, I remember thinking there were so many elements she had not completed that there was no way she could earn enough points to get a good grade on the project. Does she deserve to fail? Simply because she started at a lower point than our students. For her, in this project, it was truly the best she could do. She was so proud of herself for figuring it out. I was so proud that she stuck it out for weeks and never gave up, even when she knew where her project was compared to the rubric. Is that failure? Is that success? Make sure your rubric allows for students to start at different levels of experience. Just because your advanced students already have a skill set does not mean they should be getting all high grades. Just because someone struggles does not necessarily mean they should have low grades. It's a huge grey area that you will have to navigate as a project-based teacher. I don't think there is an easy answer. But there are ways to make lemonade from lemon all day long.

Simon Sez, "No Sage on the Stage"

Ok, the ideas here are gonna really challenge the status quo. Despite evidence which suggests that lecture is the least effective teaching tool, it is still very entrenched and prominent in our education system. I am not here to battle other discipline pedagogy, but in the CS classroom, a different approach can allow you to reach your students in ways like you have never seen. A traditional classroom flow is lecture, homework, lecture, homework, quiz, review, test. Repeat until the textbook is complete. There is so much energy around CS and technology...don't let the design and flow of your class be the exact opposite of that. Just because a teacher says it during class does not mean it was received by the students. Just because the teacher goes over a topic during class and students took notes does not mean it was learned. There is more than one way for a student to acquire knowledge. *Don't fall into the trap of thinking the only way they can get information is by being told.* Encourage and trust that your students can figure things out on their own in many cases. *That kind of learning is a different experience. In fact, they crave it.* In Jurassic Park, we learned from Dr, Grant, "....T-Rex doesn't want to be fed. He wants to hunt..." For the record, OK I'll admit...I actually do lecture, just not in the traditional way. I call it "just in time" lecture and they are usually short and sweet, anywhere from one to ten minutes, but only as needed. AND I repeat that lecture several times in each project. You can use these mini lectures on occasion to show an example, explain a concept, or address complex questions, but keep them short and sweet, get the point, and then stop.

One of the fallacies of project based learning is that the students don't learn skills. Why? I have no idea unless a project is just assigned with no thoughtfulness, no guidelines, and no skill rubric. A well designed project gives the "umbrella" under which all projects must fall. For example, in an app design class, all students have to design an app that helps a person with a mental, physical, emotional, psychological, or learning handicap or disability. The rubric is designed such that in order to complete the project, a certain skill would have to be used. This is crucial to the PBL classroom--in this scenario students see exactly why they have to learn and use a skill. That is the context you need, and it was done naturally through their project I am also careful in the proposal to challenge them to expand their proposal such that in order to complete what they propose, the teacher knows what skills will be needed, and the student will learn those as needed. In that app design class, for example, if one of the rubric requirements is that they have to use one of the sensors on the device, I'll announce, "Hey class, John wants to use voice recognition to allow audio input instead of typing. If you think you might need voice in your project, meet at the back white board in one minute." Then I will go over how the accelerometer works, look at some real examples, and see how to access it through code. What is different is that the students hearing the mini-lecture need the information and have chosen to be there.

Another alternative to lecture is to pre-record several short videos of skills, commands, concepts, or techniques that you think students may need to know. Provide a folder full of these resources. When you get those questions, students can "hear" (and re-hear) that lecture at their own pace when they need it, both in and out of class. One of the reasons why traditional lecture is less effective is simply because the students hearing it don't necessarily need the information at that time. Every semester I add to this collection of videos; they have proven to be extremely effective and valuable tools for the student, especially with 24/7 access.

Quizzes and tests

Design quizzes and tests that require students to demonstrate and use their skills. Mini projects due at the end of class are better than a paper quiz. Even let them partner! If you quiz, sometimes allow open computer, open project, open internet--whatever they need. Make the quiz something that cannot be copied or learned beforehand. The logic of this is that students can look up how to do any command in any language in just seconds on Google, so having them memorize a specific command is not the best use of their time. Actually identifying when that command is needed and then actually *using it* is important. On your quiz, have them solve a problem which requires the use of the command you want to evaluate. But, I'll ask you, "Why are you evaluating in the first place?" Is there value in the evaluation tool itself or are you just filling a gradebook column? The best evaluation tools can also be learning experiences in themselves. A student can demonstrate summative and formative learning through a wide variety of mediums. Just start to realize that traditional quizzes and tests are among the least engaging forms of evaluation.

Presentations and peer reviews

Spend time in class with students critiquing each other's projects. Students learn to give and receive feedback, both critical and positive. At the end of all projects, spend some time enjoying each other's projects. One teacher, **Dr. Melanie Wiscount**, uses an event called Gallery Walk, where students enjoy each other's projects. It is useful on many levels: firstly, it gives kids a chance to see what the others are doing. It also gives kids a chance to critique and compliment other projects, and get ideas for their own along the way. She does this "assessment" before the project is due, so students can use any feedback to enhance their own project. Students may not agree with the critiques, but they should at least consider the ideas. In each of our classes, we have one or two students each week project their project on the screen to show what they are doing, describe how they doing it, and solicit ideas and feedback. This is especially good for students who are struggling because they can see how others are approaching their projects.

Students as teachers

Students can and will be your best teachers. Embrace that. You do not need to be the all-knowing expert sage on the stage. As students learn things, either on their own through experimentation or as they are assigned specific topics to research, have them share their ideas with the class. Some of this will occur naturally if you allow student collaboration. Having a quiet computer science class stifles peer learning and teaching. Students who share their learning with the class gain respect from their peers and confidence in their own abilities. Plus, they develop valuable life skills! Especially with new teachers or inexperienced teachers, your students can help you learn new technology as well. New teachers can use this to let students help you explore projects and figure things out as you develop your curriculum.

Reflection and progress evaluation

In a project-based technology class, where you are going to have students of every possible skill-level, you want to embrace those differences. Try not to use a grading system that only allows your most talented students to make good grades. It need not be a competitive class. If a weaker student makes tremendous strides in his project, make sure the rubric reflects that. Reward them for hard work, progress, energy, effort, and dedication. Just because a student catches on quicker, or comes into the class with a higher skill set does not mean his grade should be higher.

Of course students have to demonstrate skills, concepts, ability, and understanding, but there are many ways to do that. You want to see what they can do, not necessarily just what they know. You can use self-reflective BLOGS posts for weekly progress evaluations. We use this in our longer projects, so students can reflect on their regular struggles and successes. It's important that they can talk about their project, the technology, and the code behind it. At the end of a project, I also like reflective comments because it gives students a chance to look back over the project, both in context of the Computer Science class, as well as their own performance.

Another effective tool you can try is to have students complete the sentence, "This week I will __ ." At the end of the week, I'll publically read each student's sentence aloud and ask each how they did. It's a great way to hold them accountable, push them, and let peers give regular feedback as well.

Additionally, in all my classes, I use a check-in system to keep students on task, focused, and making progress. While all projects are unique, many common elements can be found in all projects. Each week, students have to meet a specific set of goals in order to receive credit. Because students work at different rates and struggle in different areas, I like to offer some flexibility here. On check-in day, for each student I record what was/was not accomplished. Students can earn back *any* lost points the next day by showing me they were able to accomplish the required rubric items. Earlier in the book, in several cases studies, there were several sample rubrics. There are other examples offered later of a Reflective and Self-Grade rubric.

Project grading and self-grading

After each project, using the same rubric that they have been using for the duration of the project, have the students submit a self-graded grade calculation, along with a paragraph defending their request using the language of the rubric. You'll be amazed at the honesty and accuracy you will receive. You can use that as you evaluate and grade to make sure you are on target. I'll usually have two rubrics for this: 1) the project itself with a carefully articulated checklist of skills that need to be demonstrated in the project, and 2) self-performance grade where they evaluate their own efforts during the project. It is crucial that you define and describe exactly what an A effort looks like, as well B and C. You can reuse this performance rubric in all your classes.

If you see a difference in performance and grade calculation, that is a perfect time for a conversation. All grades are earned, not given. In a class based on effort and progress, you want to be sure your grades reflect the actual work.

Video or audio project and class evaluations: After each project, I have students submit a video/audio project evaluation where they critique the project itself by giving me advice on how I can make the project better, things I can do to help students learn better, or even critiques of the project. I allow text-based, audio, or video as medium choices. My video reflections tend to be the most useful to me. Free resources for this type of multi-media interaction include: Audacity is free on Mac and PC for audio recording, and Flipgrid allows up to five minute videos using any device with internet access. These *project* evaluations are different than the *teacher* evaluations students complete at the end of the year.

Deep code dives

One of the skills I believe that needs to be developed is the ability to talk about technology and Computer Science at a deep level. That means understanding the technology, but also how to talk about the code that drives it. One way to do this is having students submit recordings of themselves describing sections of code they have written. This forces them to really identify and understand what their code does, but also gets them comfortable with the language and vocabulary. This can also be helpful if students are using the internet for code samples and snippets. About two-three times per project, I'll have students do this. You can use something like FlipGrid if you wanna get fancy, or you can just use a dropbox or email. I have even had them call my voicemail at school to leave a recorded message describing the code.

"Deep Code Dives" has been one of the additions I am most excited about in the last few years. I am now doing it in all my classes, and I *highly* recommend it. It also gives you a chance to hear from your students and see who is really connecting with CS and "getting it."

Culminating experiences

Think about designing project-based culminating cumulative experiences in your classes. It is also crucial to give them time in class to prepare. I am suggesting this instead of an exam. My last few days of class before the final presentations are all presentation prep. We do our final presentations in the evening and make it formal. In one class, we do a "science fair" style event where students demonstrate to a large audience about various technologies. In another class, we do a parent workshop where students lead an adult through an entire project. In another class, we do a "Shark Tank" style experience where students are interviewed by numerous judges from the community. In another class, we have a team-based capstone project that lasts about three weeks. There is tremendous learning value in a culminating event that is different than an exam. Don't tell my students, but I also get them to spend *significantly* more time, energy, and effort on these preparations and events than they ever did on paper exams. They "buy" into these events because they are authentic. I still have alumni talk to me about the presentations they did. I don't hear alumni reminiscing about their multiple choice and short answer exams.

Online discussions

This class lends itself to cool videos, current events, cool gadgets, and cool ideas. The internet is full of interesting articles, videos, images, newscasts, BLOGs, chats, and other media related to technology. Bring those into your classroom each week. You want the students thinking about these ideas as often as possible, and how they can be used in various industries to address problems and innovate. These are the times where students really start to make real world connections with CS. As they develop this skill of being able to have real conversations, let them start to actually lead weekly discussions online and in person. You will be amazed how eager they are to research, share ideas, debate, and express opinions. Take advantage of that energy.

Speakers and guests

Try to have at least one speaker from industry in each of your classes. For example, if you are doing a game design section of class, find a professional game designer, whether that is in person, skype, field trip, or on the phone. Allowing the "real world" to be part of class is crucial to Computer Science. The great news is there are experts everywhere who are honored to be asked to Skype in for 30 minutes with your kids. Any nearby colleges have professors who might be valuable partners. I have yet to be turned down; I find that many successful adults are actually nervous about interacting with a middle or high school class. It's a great chance to make connections in the community as well as internationally.

Community

Reaching out

As you build your program and start to look for ways to reach out into the community, this will be your chance to connect with community and business leaders. Your students might compete in competitions, put on their own competitions, organize student-led technology demonstration events, technology fairs, or project demonstrations. Invite some of your local community leaders, academic leaders, political leaders, and business leaders to these events. Let them interact with your students. It's great for your students, your school, and great for the community as a whole to see what's happening in schools. If you are in private education, it helps get the word out how your school is forward thinking and distinguishing itself from competitors.

Especially as you explore other synchronous efforts to build up your percentage of females and diversity, you need those students to interact with successful people LIKE THEM in the world of technology. What female business leader can turn down a chance to talk with and support middle or high school girls?! What successful person of color will turn down a chance to help increase diversity in the growing CS field? You'll actually be amazed at who you might get. I don't think I have ever been turned down and we have had national and international corporation CEO regularly in our events.

You will be amazed at how many of your school's alumni are in tech-related careers. I find they are usually very excited to "give back."

Know your parents

With IT, technology, and Computer Science being part of virtually every industry on the planet, it is very likely you are going to have many of the parents of your students that you can tap for speakers, support, field trips, and internships. My experience is that most parents are proud and honored--and bend over backwards to help. So just ASK! You can use them in different ways: for example, as speaker just to talk about their experience with technology in their industry, an expert who can demonstrate a specific product, a professional who can help you manage a project that is within their space, judges for class competitions, or just as guests to see student projects and presentations.

Internships

During the academic school year, summer break, spring break, and Christmas break, there are numerous opportunities for your students to get involved with local businesses. These do not even need to be paid, but the students do need to be mentored-- your students are looking for their first chance to get real experience here. Just be clear with the partner companies to make sure they understand part of their obligation is to teach and mentor as well. They will get good results, but they will have to help students. Tap into any local businesses, academic institutions, and startups. They might have formal internship and job shadow programs. But if not, they might have some informal ways of connecting as well. Startups are always looking for free labor. Perhaps a couple of your more talented students can offer a few hours a week, unpaid for the experience. Nonprofits in town are usually tight on money and low on technical resources, so you might take advantage of that and get your students involved in anything from helping them unbox a new computer, setup a printer, connect their Wi-Fi network, or even design some software to help them manage their business. Nonprofits rarely refuse volunteer help.

Social Networking

You have heard me mention several times how vital it is that you get connected with the CS community. Earlier I listed some excellent and extremely active Facebook discussion groups. These connections are as valuable as curriculum, especially for the new teacher. These networks will be your social interaction with fellow teachers in Computer Science...helping to offset the fact that you might be the only CS teacher at your school.

Additionally, there are some excellent bloggers and Twitter users who can provide insights, project ideas, pedagogy analysis, current trends, and other CS topics and events. The potential for networking is incredible. Especially with the Silo effect we talked about earlier, these online communities are the lifeblood for many people in CS.

Obviously, this list is very dynamic and new people come into the field every few months. It is meant to be representative of the types of people you can connect with. Reach out and connect as often as you can.

CS Tweeters

There are hundreds of active CS tweeters in the twitter world. Here are just a few to get you started in this. Incredibly active, responsive, and supportive community. GET ON TWITTER now! This social media is for current events, great links to article and videos, pictures of success in the classroom, collaboration opportunities, and idea generation:

Alfred Thompson, @AlfredTwo, High school computer science teacher, textbook author, curriculum consultant

Anthony Owen, @AnthonyOwenADE, Arkansas's State Director of Computer Science, incredible state level efforts

Bob Irving, @birv2, Middle school CS teacher. #MIEExpert, Raspberry Pi Certified Educator, Minecraft Global Mentor

Computer Science Teachers Association, @csteachersorg, CSTA is a national membership organization for computer science teachers.

CSforALL Consortium, @CSforALL, The CSforALL Consortium is a network of providers, schools, funders, & researchers working to support expanding access to CS education for all students.

CS for All Teachers, @CsforAllTchrs, A virtual community for PK-12 computer science teachers & those who support #CSForAll.

CSNYC, @csnyc, NYC Foundation for Computer Science Education: ensuring all students in the NYC public school system have access to CS education through #CS4All initiative.

David Renton, @drenton72, Lectures in Games Development at West College Scotland. Microsoft MVP & Innovative Expert Educator. BAFTA YGD nominee

Dawn DuPriest, @DuPriestMath, Computer Science and Electronics teacher, Feminist, and Maker. 2012 Poudre School District Teacher of the Year. Allen Distinguished Educator 2016.

Jackie Corricelli, @mrscorricelli, APCS teacher and trainer of AP CS teachers

Julie Sessions, @Julie_Sessions, Accomplished author and influencer, specializing in curriculum development with a special love of younger students and computer science/ technology /science integration. Excels in project-based classroom

Mark Guzdial, @guzdial, Professor in Interactive Computing at Georgia Tech, CS Ed Researcher

Mike Zamansky, @Zamansky, Full of life and ideas about Computer Science education, but does not mind taking the politically incorrect road-less travelled approach

National Council for Women in Technology, @NCWIT, Revolutionizing the face of technology by increasing the participation of girls and women.

Rebecca Dovi, @superCompSci, She is on a mission that every student should have access to computer science. Co-founder @codeVirginia

Steven Floyd, @stevenpfloyd , HS CompSci/CompEng Teacher '17 Award for Teaching Excellence in CompSci. - M.Ed. - eLearning course writer and developer.

TeachCode, @TeachCode, supporting K12 educators in teaching computer science and leading the movement to make CS a part of every young person's education.

Vicky Sedgwick, @VisionsByVicky, K-8 Tech Teacher, Tech Trainer, Edcamp Organizer, #csk8 Chat Moderator, CSTA 2016-17 Standards Revision Task Force Member

Aaron Maurer, @coffeechugbooks, Founder of @212steamlabs, STEM Lead for AEA 9, thought provoker, educator boundary pusher

Ria Galanos, @cscheerleader, advocate for CS education and diversity in tech

Steve Isaacs, @mr_isaacs, Teacher|Video Game Development, Outstanding Teacher | PBS Lead Digital Innovator NJ|@brainpop CBE | Microsoft Innovative Educator | #minecraftmentor | @minefaire producer

CS Bloggers

This is yet another different type of social media. There are hundreds of bloggers, so don't think the following list is complete; I just wanted to get you started. Bloggers are able to expand on ideas more than in other social media and their posts stay up longer giving you a chance to find time to read. These bloggers update weekly or monthly

Edutopia	https://www.edutopia.org/
Mark Guzdial	http://computinged.wordpress.com
Garth Flint	http://gflint.wordpress.com/
Mike Zamansky	http://cestlaz.github.com/
Doug Bergman	http://innovativeteacher.org/
Alfred Thompson	http://blog.acthompson.net
Vicki Davis	http://www.coolcatteacher.com/
Jim Pike, Code Rev	https://www.coderevkids.com/blog/
Unplugged CS	http://csunplugged.org/teachers/
Laura Blankenship	http://www.geekymomblog.com/
Miles Berry	http://milesberry.net/
Dawn DuPriest	
	https://codinginmathclass.wordpress.com/
Steve Isaacs	
	http://gamesandlearning1.blogspot.com/

Alan O'Donohoe

https://teachcomputing.wordpress.com/

CSTA

http://advocate.csteachers.org/

Jill Westerland

http://www.abstractingcs.com/abstractingcs-blog/

Rasmussen College, School of Technology

http://www.rasmussen.edu/degrees/technology/blog/

Section Four

Ways to Enhance your CS Program

Competitions and Awards

These are a great way to get your more advanced students involved in special ways and also help them get recognized for their talents. It is also a chance to give your school some recognition and give the teacher a chance to network as well. As Computer Science becomes more a part of our schools, we'll see competitions sprout up everywhere. These are so engaging for kids, and the collaborative nature provides valuable real-world business skills. I highly recommend exploring this with your students. Below are several more popular events to get you started. This list is by no means complete, so investigate on your own to give your students these additional chances to compete.

Cyber Security Competitions

Cyber CTF (Digital Capture the Flag cybersecurity challenge event): This CTF competition aims to encourage and promote interest in cybersecurity. United States-based high school and undergraduate college students will have the opportunity to compete in cybersecurity challenges to gain real-life experience and win national coverage to make a huge impact on our cyber talent pipelines.

PicoCTF (in March): This is a team-based Capture the Flag online event. It is a computer security "game" targeted at middle and high school students. The game consists of a series of challenges centered around a unique storyline where participants must reverse engineer, break, hack, decrypt, or do whatever it takes to solve the challenge. The challenges are all set up with the intent of being hacked, making it an excellent, legal way to get hands-on experience.

Cyber Patriot (Nov - Apr): The National Youth Cyber Education Program was created by the Air Force Association (AFA) to inspire K-12 students toward careers in cybersecurity or other science, technology, engineering, and mathematics (STEM) disciplines critical to our nation's future. At the center of CyberPatriot is the National Youth Cyber Defense Competition. The competition puts teams of high school and middle school students in the position of newly hired IT professionals tasked with managing the network of a small company.

CSAW: (Nov) This is the largest student-run cyber security event in the world, featuring international competitions, workshops, and industry events.

Programming Competitions

ACSL American Computer Science League: http://www.acsl.org/ This is a math heavy competition offered throughout the year for students of all ages. There is a written math section as well as an individual programming component as well. Competitions are offered four times per year.

USA Computing Olympiad: This is an Oct - April competition that has a math and Computer Science focus. It has a variety of self-determined levels, group and individual components.

Lockheed-Martin CodeQuest:
https://www.lockheedmartin.com/us/who-we-are/community/codequest.html : Code Quest is an annual computer programming competition where teams of two-threeHigh School students each work together for 2.5 hours to solve problems by using JAVA, Python, VB.net, C, and/or C++ programming to complete the "quest." The problem set consists of 15-20 challenging problems created by Lockheed Martin engineers and computer programmers. These competitions are in cities all across the country.

Local colleges and companies often hold competitions to engage high schoolers in Computer Science. They use these competitions as recruiting tools, but they are excellent opportunities. Contact regional universities and colleges directly.

Robotics Competitions

Vex Robot Competitions has team-based events starting in 4th grade and going all the way through college. They have local, regional, national, and international levels. There can be some costs associated with this.

FIRST Lego League has leagues and competitions for ages as early as age six and going all the way through the twelfth grade. There can be some costs associated with this kind of team, but there are also many scholarships available. They have local, regional, national, and international levels.

WLRC: Especially for ages six-twelve to compete in a series of collaborative coding challenges

NASA compiles a list of robotic events across the country: https://robotics.nasa.gov/events/competitions.php

Other Competitions

NCWIT: National Council for Women in Technology. Oct - Nov is the application window for ninth-twelfth grade girls to submit applications for state and national level recognition. This organization is focused on supporting and recognizing female students and teachers who are engaged with Computer Science. It provides an incredible network for girls as they grow into this field.

CSTA Cutler-Bell Prize in High School Computing is open to all high school seniors. Up to four students are recognized with a $10,000 prize to be used towards college tuition.

Section Five

A look inside our CS program

My school, Porter-Gaud School, has always embraced innovation and exploration in Computer Science. Through that environment and support, we have been able to create a nationally recognized 1st - 12th CS program. In this section of the book, I'll "deep dive" into our high, middle, and elementary school programs, giving you details of every aspect of the programs to give you a taste of our motivations, goals, and projects.

Upper School, Doug Bergman, 20+ years of experience.

9th Grade

9th graders attend class five times per week for a semester-long required course. Average class size seventeen.

The projects I do in the 9th grade were all described in depth in the CASE STUDIES sections earlier in the book.

The "final exam" is more like a science fair where student pair up in teams of two to prepare a demonstration and presentation about two of the topics used during the semester. On presentation evening, there will be fifty+ parents into the library as students demonstrate and present numerous times. Students spend the entire week before preparing for the event. During the event, students have to record their best presentation for grading. Their table display and video presentation count as their final exam. This activity is a great opportunity for parents to see their children perform in an academic setting. It is also looks great for your department, faculty, and school.

At the completion of the 9th grade class, students can apply to be in our CS program which continues each year until graduation. In a typical grade-size of about one hundred students, we usually get about forty applications. I think there is value in a short private interview with each student, a form to fill out, and a set of questions responses they have to complete.

10th Grade

10th graders attend class five times per week in a one semester elective honors level class either. Class size averages about seventeen students. It's the first time students have chosen to be in the class, so it allows you to push the envelope on projects because you know they want to be here.

A typical week begins with two students introducing that week's discussion question that *they* will be leading. Once the projects have started, a typical class would start with me addressing the class for a few minutes with reminders of upcoming check-ins, expectations and motivations for homework, and clarifications of any project's rubric items. It is also a time for students to share a couple successes or failures that others can learn from. If there is a skill or concept that many students are struggling with, this is when we would discuss it.

Xbox Game Design, *technology: C-sharp, Visual Studio, Monogame, game controller, dance pad*

Students learn to use a professional level language through an educational game. Students will program several hundred or even thousand lines of code. We spent the first few days introducing the IDE programming environment, playing with code, looking at the self-help resources that are available, and reviewing a few previous semester projects. These projects will span numerous weeks, so it is worth spending a few days researching and proposing. Students design an advanced multi-level game whose ultimate goal is to teach something, so it has to have purpose. There are weekly graded check-ins throughout the project to keep them on track and making progress. In order to think about games differently, we watch a TED talk by Jane McGonigal about "serious" games. Homework assignments in this section involve playing/critiquing actual educational games on sites such as brainpop.com, researching the gaming industry and new gaming technology, and looking at alternative style games and games feedback. We usually have a speaker from game design industry to talk about professional game design. Using Monogame, games can be exported to Android, Mac, or Windows.

Life Simulations, technology: *BlueJ Java, Finch robots*

Students learn to program in Java through a series of business and life simulation projects. After introducing the required skills, they'll spend anywhere from three to ten days on each project. There will also be a required section and an on-your-own section for each project.

- **Car driving:** Students write a program that keeps track of mileage, mpg, and trip distance of the car, as well as money from the driver. Some students choose to have visuals.

- **Robot Simulation**: Using Finch robots, students design a control panel that actually controls movement of the bots. We have students simulate battery level. Each movement has an energy-cost. Battery can be recharged with solar panel (simulated by using a flashlight on light sensors).

- **iPod music player:** Using an array to store songs, students write the user interface and all iPod functionality, including display and actual playing of music.

- **The Game of Life:** Students study John Conway's cellular automaton simulation. It's an advanced double dimension array assignment that is one of the best ways to learn real algorithms.

- **Photo manipulation:** This is a great assignment that allows students to see how a program like Photoshop works. The idea came from college board AP "Picture" project. Students will actually write their own image filters such as grayscale, color replace, or negate. They will also implement a "green screen" system by coding their own version of a "copy-paste" function that replicates a section of one image to another.

- **Horse Racing simulation:** This is an awesome array project for advanced programming classes. It teaches them how to manipulate and iterate through an array while designing a multi-horse visual horserace!

- **Monopoly:** I've been doing this project for fifteen+ years. It is one of the largest and most complex projects they'll do in our CS program. The idea is to create a digital version of the board game. The reason I love it so much is that in order to implement the game, it requires almost every CS skill, command, and construct that we have learned so far. I still have alumni who refer to this when we meet.

Weekly Discussion: In teams of two, students take turns each week leading a discussion about a technology they find interesting. They'll find a short video or article to introduce their topic and then post several question prompts that others will discuss all week. This is an especially active discussion because students are expected to challenge each other, and must respond to any challenge question.

Culminating Event: The **"final exam"** is a two-hour session where students guide their parents through an entire project chosen by the student. In the week before, they practice teaching with classmates. They are allowed to bring a Cheat-Tweet (144 characters anything they want to write), but students are not allowed to use any notes, touch the keyboard or mouse during the actual teaching session...although they can *say* anything they want. I want to see them demonstrate their skills, communicate their understanding, and troubleshoot problems that arise. For grading, students will select their best ten minutes of their session for me to grade. I want to hear logical and helpful explanations of code, responses to questions, and troubleshooting strategies. Parents really love this for several reasons, and it is also a great chance to let the community see what happens in your school.

11th Grade

11th graders attend class five times per week for one semester elective honors level class

A typical week begins with my addressing the class for a few minutes with regular reminders of BLOG reflection question prompts, describing that week's "business" assignment, student project demonstrations, and having a few students do their thirty-second-elevator-pitch in front of the class. Every Monday, students submit a "What I am going to accomplish this week" email that I ask them about publically again on Friday. This helps hold them accountable to themselves and their peers. It also helps slacker students realize they need to step it up. One evening each week, they'll reflect on successes and stumbling blocks through the last week. Every third week they submit a video of their project in action, so I can see exactly their progress. During the early phases of the project, I invite real entrepreneurs to talk with each student to help them fine-tune their project ideas and find real world value. This has been a great help for me! Towards the end of the semester, I invite fellow faculty in as practice-judges in a few Shark Tank rehearsals.

Motion-Gesture-Position Skeleton Tracking,

Technology: *Motion Capture 3D camera (such as Kinect), Visual Studio C-Sharp*

We spend the first few days just experimenting with the technology to understand exactly what it is. We'll look at previous projects and even have previous students demonstrate their project to the current class to give them a taste of what's to come. The starter project allows them to run a "Hello World" to see how to setup camera, get connected, access skeletal data, and run the program. For a couple of days, we'll explore code, explore thinking about coding in 3D (which is something they have never done), add and modify code so they see how things work. This is a four-month project, so it is crucial that you spend a few days proposing projects. I rarely accept the first proposal because I want to them to *really* want to do something. They can choose any type of experience that involves movement, motion, gestures and that a marketable product can be built around-- there has to be social value in their idea. Each week, we'll study the business side of Computer Science and bringing their prototype to market, either to make profit or to get lots of people to use.

Past projects included injury rehabilitation, self-defense training, sport "swing" analysis, stress detection, interview behavior analysis, flight simulator, DUI sobriety test, concussion detection, dangerous driving simulator (texting, drunk driving, ice, rain), crime scene analysis, and even a full body music instrument. There are weekly graded check-ins throughout the project to keep them on track and making progress. They have to think about whole-body navigation and how to interact and navigate. What I love about this project is that it is truly the longest project they will work on in their high school career.

Projects of that length allow you to lead that class differently. You can let students explore something for days without fear of not getting through the chapter or getting in the quiz before the test. I can let students spend time trying something that may not work (I am usually wrong because they *do* find a way), but can encourage them to keep plugging away at it. That fear of failure is simply non-existent in this class.

There is weekly homework related to the business side of the project. These assignments include researching the existing market, SWOT analysis, creating advertising and promotion strategies, brainstorming marketing, numerous 30-second elevator pitches, alternative use brainstorming, identification of target audience, interviews with and demonstrations to industry expert related to their project, and competitive analysis. In addition, each week students reflect on their own learning and progress in a weekly BLOG post. This is important in long projects to "smell the roses along the way." We also have weekly discussion questions related to alternative technologies.

I wanted to share the project-grading rubric we use for our skeleton motion-capture project (one project all semester). This rubric has two components, which is crucial in a project-based environment. One is for the elements of the project itself and the other is to give students a chance to communicate about their own performance and effort. Having students self-reflect and self-grade is a valuable experience for both you and the student! All students additionally provide a five-minute video-demonstration, where they show off all elements of the project. This helps reduce conflict and uncertainty in expectations and grading.

Part I rubric: Project elements

10 = highly satisfactory or exceeded your/my expectations 6 - 9 = good in some ways, but room for improvement 0 - 5 = did not attempt or meet expectations

(explain any number as appropriate)

20% Program Flow and Engagement
_____Most Important: reflects 4 months of rigorous work and progress
_____Program works as expected without errors and bugs
_____It is clear what kind of program it is and who it is for
_____It is clear what the tasks and goals are
_____It is clear how to manipulate the flow of program
_____It is clear how to do what we are being asked to do
_____It is engaging, fun, interactive
_____It does what it says it does in the way we would expect

20% Human Computer Interface: Gesture-based Navigation

_____Most Important: reflects 4 months of rigorous work and progress
_____How to navigate is clear
_____How to navigate is easy to do as expected
_____Successfully navigates through program
_____No "accidental" page changes, delays, consequences
_____Appropriate choice of gesture & skeletal position/movement
_____Motions relate to context of program.

20% Design and Layout
_____Most Important: reflects 4 months of rigorous work and progress
_____Title makes sense in context
_____Appealing to the eye
_____Screens are laid out well to take advantage of screen size
_____Text is clear and prominent against the background
_____Wording is grammatically correct, no spelling errors, visible, clear & concise
_____Object and placement of objects on screen makes sense and is logical
_____Any DEBUG printing is removed
_____Any unneeded text display is removed

20% Interactive User Feedback

_____Most Important: reflects 4 months of rigorous work and progress

_____Feedback makes sense in context of project

_____Feedback is useful and appropriate

_____Displayed prominently

_____It is obvious if we are doing well/towards goals

_____It is obvious if we are not doing as well as intended

20% Subjective

_____Most Important: reflects 4 months of rigorous work and progress

_____Clever, engaging, accurate, & appropriate

_____Main Menu/Welcome Screen

_____Appropriate for target audience

_____Program is as complete and thorough and complex as possible

_____Quality and appropriateness of Screen layout and Design

_____Quality and appropriateness of images/video

_____Quality and appropriateness of sounds effect/audio

_____Engaging/interactive experience?

_____Educational Value, Market Value, or Potential Value to Target audience

_____Reached the original stated program proposed project(from BLOG)

_____Reached reasonable completion point based on time spent in/out of class

Part II rubric: Personal Performance, Accomplishment, and Effort Rubric

The reason for having this type of rubric in addition is so that students actually think about their own learning. In a project-based class when the project is the center of the learning, students can get caught up in just making progress without thinking about, or giving themselves credit, for accomplishing many great things along the way. The goal of the entire class would be that students spent a long time working with a technology that was foreign to them, and through hard work, determination, effort, trial and error, and persistence...they can accomplish something great. It may or may not be exactly what they set out to do; in some cases, it might be far beyond that; in other cases, they found out along the way that their project had some fundamental flaws; in other cases, the project morphed into something else. All of that is ok as long as it is intentional.

Self-Performance Evaluation

Students: Considering the below rubric, assign yourself a grade and defend it using the vocabulary included in the rubric above.

Scoring is defined as:
A+(98), A(95), A-(92)
B+(88), B(85), B-(82)
C+(78),C(75), C-(72)

A: All elements of my project are implemented above expectations. The completed project reflects tremendous amounts of work and accomplishment resulting in a project incredibly well done and exceeding expectations of myself, my teacher, and the project rubric. As needed, I asked question from my peers or teacher as well as researched on my own. I was able to learn from my mistakes and build upon failures. I spent time outside of class as needed. I was able to commit an average of 4-5 hours per week towards class. This project reflects my best effort, progress, and performance. I am extremely proud of how this project turned out.

B: Most elements of my project are implemented satisfactorily. The completed project reflects sufficient effort to complete the project at the expected level both as expected of myself, my teacher, and the project rubric. I accomplished some of what I set out to do. I found myself getting stuck in some of the same places repeatedly. I occasionally got help from my peers or teacher as well as researched on my own as needed. I was able to commit an average of 4-5 hours per week towards class in most cases, but there were several weeks I did not. I was able to spend some time outside of class, but more was needed. This project reflects my good, but not my best effort, progress, and performance. I am satisfied with and proud of most aspects of the project, although there were areas that needed improvement

C: Some elements of project are implemented satisfactorily. The completed project did not meet expectations of myself, my teacher, or rubric guidelines, and/or reflects insufficient effort to complete the project at a satisfactory level. I did not accomplish what I set out to do. I did not usually ask questions from my peers or teacher or research on my own. I was not able to commit an average of 4-5 hours per week towards class most weeks. I did not spend time outside of class as needed. This project does not reflect my best effort, progress, and performance. The finished project is not something I am proud of.

Culminating Event: Shark Tank "Final Exam"

Their final exam experience is unlike anything they have ever done. Several judges from the community are invited to our event, which allows students to present, demonstrate, and "sell" their product in an effort to get $1000 from any one of the judges. Judge might be entrepreneurs, business executives, programmers, marketing directors, presidents of schools, alumni, and course several CS teachers. It is very unlikely any student could have expected what it might be like, which is part of why we include such an authentic audience. We want them to think about the entire experience as a learning opportunity, recognizing the importance of both the successes and stumbling blocks they had during the presentations. They will not only show the functionality of their projects, but also the value and marketability of it. Their "persuasive" arguments can also play a part. It is not always they best projects which succeed that night, it is the best overall presentations. Many will make changes to their final project based on the experience of the evening. This rubric also allows the chance to make suggestions for next year's class. Here is the final reflective assignment they have:

> Describe your thoughts about the experience (what was different-unexpected/expected?)
> What would you change about your presentation or preparation if you did it again?
> What did you enjoy? What did you NOT enjoy? Why?
> Who gave you money? How do you know?
> Who did NOT give you any money? How do you know?
> What was biggest "oops" of the night?
> What was biggest "OH YEAH!" of the night
> Advice for next year's students for project itself?
> Advice for next year's' students for Shark Tank?
> Advice for me to change about the event Shark Tank
> Advice for me to change about project or class design?

12th Grade

12th graders attend class 5 times per week for a full year elective honors level class. Class size is about 12 students.

Swift App Development, Technology: X-Code, Swift:
Students learn various types of app development projects such as shopping lists, encryption scheme de/cipher, dice throwing simulation, a vending machine simulation, and a calculator. Each week there is a homework assignment in Playground which allows them to explore code not being used in class. Projects are designed to give them exposure to common constructs, data structures, and skills needed in advanced app development.

Cybersecurity, Technology: Virtual Box, Linux and Windows server images, CTF server

Students work their way through skills and commands related to several elements of attack and defense, cryptology, and networking. They'll participate in a local Capture the Flag (CTF) event, and contribute their own challenge for their own CTF. Class is a combination of discussion, demonstration, small and large projects usually done in teams of two. We use virtual network software to allow students to setup and design networks and control networking equipment. They explore live network traffic with industry tools and even watch documentaries about large scale exploits. Throughout the semester, we have professional security experts in to speak about current trends and stories. Throughout this section, students respond to weekly case studies about significant cyber incidents. Our Cybersecurity team members assist in class preparation as well as teaching the class. The section culminates with students in pairs researching and creating a video edu-documentary about a virus, vulnerability, attack, or other cyber related event. They are required to find and explain the code behind the event as well as the significance.

Capstone, Technology, CoDrone, Arduino C++.
The drone project is one of our most fun and challenging projects. It is also the last project the students will do as part of our program, so we like that is something "out of the box." Teams of three students explore drones. Students use all the physical dimensions: drones fly up, down, left, right, forward, back...but there will be inconsistencies and challenges to deal with such as battery strength, propeller angle, height, and airflow.

The autonomous component of the capstone piece requires them to program the drone to complete challenges that mimic real life scenarios such as military reconnaissance flights, inner city between buildings, farm-land circumference, Amazon delivery services, and medical supply delivery.

The manual control component is a set of obstacles and challenges using the remote control and requires a great deal of practice. Challenges include wild-fire reconnaissance, timed surveillance, object tracking, and pre-recorded instruction following.

What I love about drones is that there are so many challenges with drone flight programming that there is never a straightforward solution to any challenge. Students have to be very flexible.

The third component is a research component on the physics of drone flight and an in-depth investigation any industry's use of drones. The final 2 days of the project is a Team Drone Olympics competition, which includes challenges such as the 100-yard dash, Target Practice, Synchronized Flying, Rugged Maniac Obstacle race, and Hot Air Balloon to Outer Space

Interview Project: One of the most successful projects in our Computer Science program is our senior year Interview project. Students are challenged to reach out into the business world and make contact with a person in an industry that have interest in. They can aim as high as they like. They will use numerous communication tools such as email, LinkedIn, Facebook Messenger, Instagram DM, Twitter, phone calls, hand-written letters, office visits, Skype. They will try direct and indirect lines of communication to try to connect with their person of choice. Some of those attempts are unsuccessful, but excitingly most are not---most end up not only making initial contact, but also having incredible experiences. They learn about formal business communication and about professional scheduling. They learn how to research a person and an industry. They will actually interview a professional in person, on the phone or on video. We have had students get interviews with international CEOs and other high level executives of people at huge organizations such as Apple, Blackbaud, GoldieBlox, McDonald's, ESPN, and even the United States Gov't. We've also had great experiences with numerous start-ups and small business owners interviews as well. This kind of project connects Computer Science to the real world in ways that simply cannot be done in the classroom. Students present to the class about their interview and write a final reflection piece about the experience.

Rebecca was so proud of her interview with Tim Cook at Apple: www.aspirations.org/blog/innovator-innovator-apple-ceo-tim-cook-interviewed-high-school-senior-rebecca-kahn

Middle School, Bob Irving, 15+ years of experience

5th and 6th graders come to class three times a week for nine week required course, forty-five minute each class.

Microbit: Students learn to use LED display output, accelerometer, and buttons to design their own creations. The project puts them in "deep cover" as spies, requiring them to communicate only with their trusty Microbits.

Kodu: After experimenting and exploring, students create their own 3D worlds and an actual game using the 3D drag 'n drop development tools. What are project parameters? Students have a narrative background, create a world that matches that background, then learn event-based programming, score-keeping, and multiple levels.

Circuit Playground: Students expand on what they learned with Microbit and take it to the next level. A variety of projects require them to use LED's, motors, sensors, sound, and art all on a chip a bit larger than a quarter.

Dash Robots: Introduction to beginner level robotics using block-based coding to access simple motors and sensors. Students competed in Robot Olympics as teams coded their bots for races, obstacle courses, and even tic-tac-toe!

7th and 8th graders take class 5 times per week for 9 week required course

MindStorm Lego Robots*: After a couple days experimenting and exploring, students complete several robotic challenges, including at least one on-your-own project. The challenges mirror the tasks that the TUG medical robot used in hospitals does. The actual rubric is provided below. Students also build a multi-level game in Scratch.

Minecraft Python Programming: After a couple days experimenting and exploring, students complete several "Hack Pack" challenges, including at least one on-your-own project. For example, students write the code to detect a certain material under the current block. They start with constructing buildings with code, teleporting, then move on to events, so that the environment responds to the player, finishing up with drawing with turtles in the Minecraft world.

Raspberry Sonic Pi: Students explore interactive music by manipulating variables in Ruby. They do live DJing with code! The instant audio feedback helps them understand the impact and relationships of variables as well as looping and conditional statements. Students each present their best "song" to the class in the concert on the final day.

HTML: Students get their first taste of text based coding as they explore simple HTML statements. We use HTML because of the instant visual feedback and simple commands. Students spend several days creating a two-page personal website.

*Sample Rubric for 7th Grade Robotics

Here is a great example of an excellent Middle School level rubric for the open-ended robotics section. There are specific tasks, but still lots of freedom in how those tasks are accomplished. Additionally, there is a design-your-own challenge at the end. In the Computer Science classroom, this is the gold you should be shooting for. We are using the Lego Mindstorm robot series.

Your robot is a medical bot, doing very important work in a hospital. It is called the TUG robot. Its main job is to deliver medications, blood, and tissue products to doctors, nurses, and patients, freeing medical staff to spend more time taking care of patients.

Successfully completing challenges 1-4 earns you a 90. Want to level up? Do challenge #5!

You may do them in any order you like.

To do this job successfully, it must be able to do the following challenges:

1. Obstacle Detection and Avoidance -- your TUG bot must be able to sense people, objects, and other obstacles and get around them as it moves through the hallways. In some cases, these deliveries are about saving lives, so they have to do it quickly and accurately! You've got 3 challenges to show it can do that.
    1.1. Maneuver past an obstacle in the hospital hallway.
    1.2. Detect the nurse's station, stop, and tell them that the delivery has arrived.
    1.3. Display a hazard signal in its display to let people know that some of the cargo could be dangerous.
2. Detect the line. A black line in the hallway indicates a room on the right or left. Your TUG bot must be able to detect the line accurately, turn to see if the door is open. If the door is open, it goes through the door. If not, it turns and maneuvers back down the hallway until it detects another

black line, then checks for an open door again.
3. Backup detection. Your TUG robot must sense obstacles and people behind it.
If it touches someone or something behind it, it should move forward.
4. Bluetooth: TUGs will send a Bluetooth message to another robot that it must return to pick up emergency supplies. It must immediately turn around and come straight back to the sending robot.

#5 DESIGN YOUR OWN CHALLENGE.

Elementary School, Dr. Julie Sessions, 25+ years of experience

Julie used her experience as an elementary teacher to fit Computer Science into the curriculum in grades one to four. While not possible at every school, she recommends one of the most important things to do in order to get Computer Science into elementary school classrooms is to be willing to have a person who is dedicated to getting things started. For example, have a media specialist or technology integrator; you just need someone who can take the lead, figure some things out, put some things together so the teachers can hit the ground running. Maybe that person is a teacher willing to spend some time on it. Regardless of who does it, in order to best train some teachers in Computer Science, they'll need someone who is able to research technology, figure out what would work best in your school, train the teachers to be comfortable using the technology, and actually prepare that first lesson plan, and even be willing to sample teach. I know that sounds like a lot, but keep in mind at this level, the technology -both hardware and software - are very simplistic, so it does not take long to get familiar. An hour of training is usually more than enough. Julie does this preparation and helps the teachers in that first classroom experience with the students. After that, she says they are able to use it on their own. And she can go off to another set of teachers. In the beginning, she said her best successes to introduce Computer Science came in the science department, since they are already used to working with equipment and materials.

In each grade 1st - 4th, our school uses CODE.ORG curriculum which is all online and is 100% managed by CODE.ORG, so it works on iPad, Tablet, laptop, or even mobile phone. The system remembers exactly where each student is, so each time they log in, they can continue where they left off. Each year's curriculum is designed to be about 20 hours in length, and is meant to be used over the course of the entire year. In our school classes, students can code every day in homeroom or in some other regular meeting times. Julie is extremely proud that they used to spend that time doing paper worksheets; now they are coding hands-on! Throughout any day, when they finish work early, they used to be allowed to read or write on their own...now some grade levels have added coding as an additional choice.

With the CODE.ORG curriculum, teachers can also easily monitor the entire class progress from a single page. The curriculum is meant to be self-paced and age appropriate. Throughout the curriculum are a variety of diverse people introducing concepts and explain upcoming code challenges. Teachers love the interface because it is the exact same for all elementary grades, which means it's consistent for teachers as well as students.

Throughout the year, there are additional opportunities for students to learn STEM and Computer Science. For example, a group of 12th grade girls volunteer their time for CS and STEM activities all year. Each winter, the entire school spends a few days in "Beyond the Books" where students can select a program in which they will spend three days. The Computer Science programs on coding and design have become the most popular choice each year.

The science classes are incorporating robots into their classes twice per week for several weeks using the Dash robots and We-Do robotics. Students build and program the robots to perform tasks related to the current class topic, for example recycling. Physics and math experiments also work well with robots, like programming a robot to kick a ball an exact distance. Additionally, the 4th grade started using Hopscotch and Scratch Jr. which are used in game design. In fact, the teachers were looking for some an alternative means of evaluation, so they began doing entire games designs *instead of a test* in order to evaluate topics such as ecosystems (3rd grade) and the brain (4th grade). Students designed and programmed an interactive mapping of the brain using the same vocabulary as they learned in class and mapping was actually the final assessment. Students designed and built entire ecosystems using LEGO, and at the end of the project, each student 3D printed one of the objects for their design. Computer Science at any age allows student to move up Bloom's Taxonomy as they demonstrate and apply understanding of ideas, vocabulary, and concepts they learned. At the completion of their projects, each group AirPlays (sends) their project to the projector to present to class, and grading can be done simultaneously.

Because things can sometimes go wrong or break, Julie created a bank of helpful resources including online forums, Q&A sections, phone support, and especially a community of fellow teachers. This community of teachers that use software in the elementary ages is extremely collaborative and supportive of helping one another. Not surprisingly, students actually troubleshoot and solve most problems. Don't be shocked if several of your students assume the teaching role to help classmates--this happens all the time.

Worth noting is that more and more students are coming into the classes already familiar with these programs. They are finding these types of technologies and programs because of the recent popularity of Computer Science and also initiatives such as Hour of Code.

"...but can students really learn real Computer Science?", you might ask? She had an excellent example of how students learned loops. In their Recycling section of class, they first built the trucks with Legos, then programmed the truck to pick up specific types of materials and then move to the dump. Then they go back to pick up different material and move it to the dump. Then they go back to pick up another material and move to the dump. You see the repetition. Kids see it, too. That is exactly when the teacher can introduce the concept of repeating loops and how to do that in code. Looping structures are a Computer Science construct and a learning objective in CS national standards.

What's the number one way to get your principal on board with Computer Science? Julie says without question: quite simply to let him/her actually see it happening in action. Visit another school. Work with a volunteer. The kind of learning that happens with Computer Science brings a different energy than a traditional classroom. When the principal sees it that first time, he/she will "get it." Ask any project-based CS teacher.

How will you know if your CS class or CS program has succeeded?

It's not going to be instant success, but there are certainly some signs that you are on the right track: enrollment numbers, student feedback, class evaluations, peer observations, and enrollment of next level classes, even AP scores if you offer AP in high school. Those are the obvious elements, but you can also use some additional criteria, such as variety of students enrolling, number of students who enter into technology-based majors in college, interest in outside competitions, Hours of Code, Hack-a-thons, Game-jams, or after school coding clubs. Parents will also give you good feedback if they like what they are hearing from their children. If you end up reaching out into the community businesses as recommended, then you will also see the response grow. You might get to the point where those companies are calling your school to get involved.

Some of the results you might not see for several years. For example, it may be a while until the student from your class minors in Computer Science, or who changes majors in her junior year at college, or who creates his own app or software. Some other indirect signs are the types of "academic" students who are enrolling. If you are attracting your higher-end students, then that means the reputation is one such that it is worth their time to take it. That type of student does not have the time or energy to waste on a class that is too easy or adds no value.

Perhaps some of your pre-med, business, and nursing alumni students take some programming courses just because it enhances their skills. You can take credit for some of that. There may also be value in comparing current standardized test scores with scores from before your program started. Computational thinking has an impact on all learning—definitely worth checking out.

There is just the everyday energy, engagement, and spirit of the class. Don't discount this; your gut instinct here matters and it is also one of the goals of this book. This instinct tells you when you need to make changes to an assignment, project, explanation, or resource. This means you are sensing something subtle but important—listen to it.

At least one a year, a student who dropped out of our program (or could not fit it into the schedule) comes to ask for special permission to re-join. It is a great feeling and a testament to the reputation.

The Elephant in the Room

(and the elephants banging on the door)

Hopefully you are in a school with an incredibly supportive principal in a district with incredibly supportive policies and staff. Reality for many schools means obstacles in support, scheduling, personnel, politics, policy, passion, money, and skill.

This book challenges the status quo. No question about it. As you embark on this innovative Computer Science journey, you are going to encounter naysayers, narrow-minded administrators, obtuse rules, outdated policies, traditionalists, even fellow faculty who will point out every possible reason why your project-based CS vision cannot happen.

There are admissions directors at some colleges telling the students to only take classes in core (amazingly, CS is not considered core) subjects, regardless of their passions. Some high school guidance counselors might recommend taking other classes in random subjects rather than exploring something like CS that might change their life. One of our students met with the Computer Science director at a prominent college who was blown away with her accomplishments and successes in her high school Computer Science experience, and yet was told by that same school's admissions staff that none of that mattered to her. This cannot happen. Recruit aggressively anyway.

Some schools are heavily focused on meeting state and national standards. Done correctly "within" the curriculum, standards can be powerful and supportive, but many schools tend to let standards drive the course in less-than-engaging ways. Teacher, department, and school evaluations might be solely tied to standards rather than content and learning. Especially in public schools, you are going to have to address this challenge and figure a way to use standards to *enhance* the curriculum, not *limit* it.

Computer Science is leading the way for other disciplines to change what education looks like. *Doing* is more valuable than *knowing*. *Demonstrating* is more powerful than *regurgitating*. *Hands-on* is more engaging than *hand-outs*. *Projects* are more engaging and effective than traditional *lecture*. There will be those who will fight to the death for their passive classroom environments. There will be those who give you reason after reason why CS cannot happen like this. They will challenge you that true learning can only happen if teachers tell students information and students write it down in a notebook only to give it back a week later on a test. There will be those who swear learning cannot happen without a textbook to lead the class. You will have a principal who does not know how to evaluate you. You will have district policy, which severely limits what you want to do. Your IT department may restrict what you can access or run on the computers. Do it anyway.

There will be those who are stuck on standardized testing, and everything that happens in the classroom must be direct preparation for those tests and scores. The project-based CS class is going to go against the grain. You are preparing them for the real world; the world will be their test.

The elephant in the room is that yes there are going to be many things in the way of your implementing a dynamic project-based CS program. Despite these challenges, there are teachers all over the country who are part of incredibly engaging and innovative Computer Science programs. Despite (or perhaps in spite of) those around them who might tell them no, put up obstacles, or discourage them, they have built programs that students are responding to.

Another elephant-like something you need to know is the reaction of your students to a class like this. You will find students that might not have done well in traditional classes who find connections with your class. In fact, get ready for this…talk with any project-based teachers, especially CS project-based teachers, and you will find that is very common. But it is also a double-edge sword. Students who have mastered the art of memorizing and regurgitating and have their straight As without ever *really* working are going to have to work for everything they do in your class. They are used to passively being told what they need to know and exactly how it will need to be given back. The project-based CS classroom is about as opposite of that as can be. Their project progress will depend on how much elbow grease (I really wanted to use that phrase in the book) they are willing to put into the project. This conundrum is actually very important to be aware of, so address those situations immediately. Once those students understand how your CS classroom works and how to succeed, they will embrace it.

My last elephant in the room concern is that our current measuring stick for CS in education tends to be based solely on College Board AP statistics. While this is certainly one way we can evaluate certain aspects, it is NOT a complete picture. There are many high schools that have introductory CS classes, intermediate CS classes, IB programs, dual credit CS classes, advanced non-AP classes, software design classes, robotics classes, and independent maker labs. We need to include these. CS is finding its way into middle schools all over the country with incredible success. Elementary schools throughout the U.S. and the rest of the world are seeing incredible success bringing CS into classrooms. I'd like to see us develop a better system by which we determine how we are doing as CS becomes a real part of education. As teachers empower themselves by designing their own curriculum or use combinations of several available curricula, we also want to include those efforts as part of our measurement.

National organizations such as CSTA have connections with CS teachers of all kinds, all grade levels, all backgrounds, and all types of schools. The information those teachers can provide helps us understand where we are in the bigger picture, so we can help those same teachers do what they do even better.

The elephants banging on the door

There are several advanced topics related to Computer Science that are probably beyond the scope of this book, but worth mentioning. If this book is received well, maybe my next one can be on the up and coming technologies and how they fit into education☺. But, I want to at least talk briefly *three* of those topics:

 Cyber Security, A.I., and Cloud Computing

These are not necessarily futuristic; they are actually already a part of our world far more than most people even realize. They each require a different and new style of thinking, another set of tools to interact, and a new vocabulary that society has to understand. So while Computer Science itself is just finding its way into our schools, we already have to be looking further out front....in order to be preparing our students for that pipeline.

Elephant 1: Cloud Computing

The major players in the Cloud Computing arena are Amazon, Microsoft, IBM, Salesforce, Oracle, and SAP. These huge companies provide systems that are all part of cloud (internet-based) computing. For example, do you love you NetFlix? Love to stay in beautiful houses across the world via Airbnb? Do you use Lift for your transportation needs? Love browsing images from another world via the Mars Rover? Code.org uses cloud computing to manage the incredible increases in traffic to their site during December when millions of people login to do their Hour of Code

It is an entire shift in how technology works for an organization.

Especially with the huge demand for skills in this new area, we are seeing these companies now start to invest in K-12 Computer Science Education. For example, Amazon (who has been focused solely on the universities and colleges) has made a huge leap into the education world through a new program especially for schools called *AWS Educate*. It's designed for students to explore, earn badges, and even learn skills for a variety of cloud-jobs. There is even a student job board for internships and jobs. Teachers can use the provided content to align their curriculum with specific cloud-job skills.

Elephant 2: Cyber Security

So, we touched on this in our 12th grade project section, but I wanted to bring it up here to get your attention. With so many digital devices controlled by software and hardware, and so many of those devices being online, it provides ample opportunities for vulnerabilities that can be exploited by the bad guys. Knowing how to identify those weaknesses and security flaws and how to defend against them is a huge need in almost every industry that uses technology. And while there is some cross over, the skills needed in Cybersecurity are a different skillset from those needed in Computer Science. Knowing how to combat viruses and malware is more of need today than ever before. Universities and colleges are just now starting to offer degrees and certifications in this area, so the supply is going to fall far short of demand. It will be one of the most in-demand jobs in the coming decade. The understanding and skills of Cybersecurity need to be part of the vocabulary our students develop in K-12. NICERC (National Integrated Cyber Education Research Center) actually provides lots of great resources and even an entire free curriculum for teachers who will teach it in their classes. It's a great place to start.

Elephant 3: A.I. Artificial Intelligence

Technology has enabled us to detect, identify, record, monitor, and analyze data in ways never before even imagined. In fact, the quantity of data has almost grown to an amount that is too large for humans to make any sense out of it. A.I. is a set of tools, technologies, and algorithms that allow a computer to recognize patterns in data and even learn automatically based on new data. That's right, it actual gets smarter and learns! For example, autonomous car technology uses A.I. to help it navigate without a driver. Cancer researchers use A.I. to recognize tumors. Any industry that collects data of any kind can utilize A.I. For example, Microsoft has made its cloud-based Cognitive Services A.I. service available to the public for experimentation (https://azure.microsoft.com/en-us/services/cognitive-services/). Your advanced students can explore artificial intelligence for facial recognition, emotion detection, computer vision, natural language, and voice recognition.

Wait? What?

So, if you are reading this book thinking, "OK, we don't even have Computer Science class, and now you are telling me about this bleeding edge technology?" Part of the reason why we are where we are, with such a huge divide between our schools and the world, has been because of a huge vocabulary problem. Part of what I am hoping this book can do is address that language so we can all be thinking about and talking about the same things. But, yes as of right now, all of this leading edge stuff has been only addressed at the college level and beyond, but just as with all the other technologies, if we really expect our current students to be able to interact with, understand, and work with these technologies, we have to start earlier. We have to stop being afraid of these types of new technologies and instead let them be part of our regular conversations in education. So by the time students get to college, these words are already part of their vocabulary and perhaps even an understanding as well.

Sample CS Implementations

As inspiration, I'd like to take a deep dive into a few CS programs at other schools so you can see other perspectives of passion, ideas, and successful implementations.

Julie Hembree is an award winning elementary school teacher/librarian and feels that Computer Science isn't just a secondary subject. You'll hear her describe the amazing things she is doing in the early years (in fact she referees several of the technologies described earlier in the book).

In her own words:

"…If we want to have a work force with the skills to be competitive in the digital job arena, we need to start at in elementary school. While we can't prepare students for jobs when they are still young children, we can help them develop a foundational level of the problem solving skills and programming concepts they will need in more complex computer science courses.

We accomplish this by integrating CS into the required curriculum. For example, in first grade, the students study the habitat and animals of Antarctica. This unit requires students to read and write non-fiction text and then create a product that showcases their learning. Instead of making posters to share what they have learned, this year they programmed interactive stories using Scratch Jr. software. With partners, the students had to design their entire story from start to finish. They had to program their penguin to move, jump and share facts. When mistakes happen, as they always do, they have to work together to adjust their program and figure out the solution by reprogramming the blocks. The research and programming takes approximately thirty to forty-five minutes a day for about two weeks. Once the programming portion is complete, the partners meet with the teacher and together they review the progress they are making. The final step is a showcase where everyone can enjoy trying each other's Scratch Jr project stories to see how each partnership approaches the same assignment.

In the library, students program Bee-Bot robots to move through a sequence of steps to progress from South America on a gridded map to Antarctica. This assignment only takes a few minutes, but everyone wants to see how they can program the robot to move in a different (and maybe better?) pattern than anyone else.

Our entire school participates in the **Hour of Code** during Computer Science Week each fall. From kindergarten to fifth grade each class has the opportunity to code using the activities from code.org during their library class. Often these lessons are extended in the classroom so students can earn their Hour of Code certificate. In one of my library classes, one of my parent volunteers, who also happens to be a computer programmer, is able to work side-by-side with a fifth grade student and extend his learning beyond what I could teach. In this library class, my goal is to expose students to different types of computer science learning. Most of our lessons are short and are not graded. By taking away the fear of failure that grades often bring, students are more apt to push themselves beyond what their own boundaries. We Skyped with a teacher in Scotland who showed us how Minecraft could be used to learn geography and history. A local computer programmer used our class for some beta-testing of the BBC Micro:bits, a tiny programmable computer designed to motivate students and make coding both fun and practical. Spheros, Ozobots, and BeeBots give us robotic experiences.

By combining literacy, science, math, with computer science, students have the opportunity to engage in their learning with an eye for the future. They learn that computer science is not a topic to be feared, but rather one as important as math, reading or life science. Elementary school experiences build a foundation for the future and inspire further computer science learning." It helps that her principal, Drew Terry, is all-in with this. His approach is something I wish more administrators tool: "...*The ability for our students to explore Computer Science at an early age is paramount to our continued technological growth.*"

Dr. Melanie Wiscount is a nationally recognized high school Computer Science teacher. She helped develop an outstanding CS program at her school. Classes are an interesting blend of self-learning, project-based learning, textbook-based, and off-the-shelf curriculum. To limit software installation problems, and to ensure all students had access off-campus, she made sure all of her material and programming environments were available online. She helped her school develop an incredibly engaging and successful four year track:

> Exploring Computer Science
> AP Principles
> Cyber Security
> Advanced Video Game Design.

Students completed required work as well as demonstrated their own learning through self-defined projects. When she saw the need for a new Cybersecurity class (long before there was any curriculum available), she designed her own curriculum based exactly on how she wanted that class to flow. Students actually used her class to take the CompTIA Security+ test.

There are two elements of her program that I'd like to highlight and suggest you see if there is any value in bringing into your own classroom: **Code-Talks**: where each student explains exactly what a segment of code does. They practice with each other to prepare for the Teacher-Code-Talk. She is a believer that if you can explain it, you know it. The last two days of each programming module are what she calls *Showcases*, where students spend a class period presenting their project to fellow students, then another class visiting other student projects. In addition to the presenting skills they are practicing, it also gives them a chance to get real feedback from peers. Alpha and Beta testing and feedback are actually requirements of the final project submission.

Sean Wybrant is one of the most innovative Computer Science teachers in the United States. His philosophy about how projects are used in learning is directly in line with what we have talked about in the book. I started to paraphrase and reword his submission to me, but instead I am including a rather lengthy description of his entire program (in his own words) because it is a wealth of philosophy, examples, and ideas. He also shares the path he took to get where he is today.

Cyber Tech Studios is the name of the game design and information technology track of classes at William J. Palmer High School in Colorado Springs, CO. Students opting into the courses have the chance of working on a variety of projects with a variety of hardware. Between 2012 and 2017 we created a fully equipped game design and development studio that mirrors what industry looks like.

In CTS, students have access to live action motion capture hardware and software from Vicon, an industry leader in the mocap space, a professional isolation booth with Logic Pro for recording

> **We make software with the end user in mind.**
>
> **We create purposeful play through software that is educational and fun.**
>
> **We craft experiences for others that are inclusive.**
>
> **We are intentional in our endeavors.**
>
> **We strive to make a difference in the community.**

audio, high quality machines from Dell including Dell Precision Workstations and Alienware, virtual reality with the Oculus Rift, augmented reality with the Meta 2 Development Kit, and mixed reality with the Microsoft HoloLens. We also have Lego Mindstorm robots and Spheros for students to learn about robotics, Makey Makey input devices, 3D printing with a Flashforge Creator Pro, and a variety of other devices from Arduinos to Raspberry Pi machines. We use Autodesk 3D software (Maya, Mudbox, 3DS Max, Motion Builder, Inventor) and Adobe 2D software (Illustrator, Photoshop, Fireworks, Dreamweaver) as well as Unity, Visual Studio, MonoDevelop, Game Maker Studio, and a host of productivity applications. Students work to create educational software and games for other students to experience.

That wasn't where we started though. For many years, there was a game design and development 1 course that ran every semester and a game design and development 2 course that ran every other semester or as demand was high enough. In 2014 we began to move toward a more stable set of courses. Now our track looks like:

First Course	Follow-on Course
Game Development 1	Game Development 2
Game Design and Development 3	Game Design and Development 4
Java Programming 1	Java Programming 2
IB Computer Science 5	IB Computer Science 6
Honors Programming	Advanced Programming

(Sean)How Courses Work:

Each of these courses is a semester long and each builds on the previous courses. While each of these courses has a different name, the clear distinctions in the Game Development track are the difference between Game Development 1 and the rest of the courses. In the first course, we learn basics of coding, 3D environments, and the idea of how the programming and art assets work together. All students in Game Development 1 learn a little about the art, the programming, and the design of games. In the rest of the courses students can do more specialization. In Java Programming and IB Computer Science the students learn the basics of coding, and while they don't have to take any game development courses before taking on the task of learning coding in these ones students who do have a significant advantage. Honors Programming and Advanced Programming are independent study courses where students have more freedom and flexibility to identify projects they would like to take on with actual clients and then they work towards making software for those clients as well as creating a portfolio of their work throughout the program.

The typical schedule for a student is that they take GD1 and GD2 in their 10th grade year, GD3 and GD4 in their 11th grade year, and honors/advanced in their senior year. Sometimes students will double up on classes in their upper years and I have had some students in my room for up to three or four hours a day to work on projects.

Design Thinking is an approach to problem solving that focuses on making sure that the focus of the solution remains on what the end user and client actually need. To do this we need to make sure that we find out what that end user wants, needs, struggles with, and can use. Then, we ensure that we define the problem with all of its specific needs. Then, we ideate, which means to create many ideas - — brainstorming. Once we have created a variety of different ideas, we prototype a solution. Next, we test that solution with the end user. Next, we refine our solution based on the feedback of the end user and if necessary, we restart the process. It is possible that the end user's/client's needs will change based on the solution that we present to them. We always start with the end user in mind and we keep them in mind at every step.

(Sean)Projects:

While many people structure their courses around a discrete set of skills, we approach the process of game design and development from the perspective of outcomes. Students identify a project worth doing, and then ground that project in a type of hardware or multiple types of hardware we have at our disposal. Some of the projects we are currently working on are:

Virtual Reality Escape Rooms:

When we got the Oculus Rift for development, we decided that we would begin work on creating virtual reality escape rooms as a way to weave interesting academic content into virtual reality spaces in ways that were both fun and meaningful academically. Students are working on creating virtual environments with content that would fit into those environments and are mapping the experiences to create the kinds of content that they have been asked to know, memorize, and learn in their various academic classes. Examples of this include an environment the kids are calling Mineshaft, where the idea is that students will use their knowledge of history and geology to create a fun environment where your ability to escape is based on your understanding of the ways that those content areas and economics work. Another is an environment based on an art museum where you have to know about how circuits work and the ways that tumblers work to solve puzzles that allow you to "steal" pieces of art from history…and in the process learn a little about art history. Another is the creation of a Native American cliff dwelling, which has opened conversations in classes about cultural appropriation versus cultural appreciation.

Students can get started working on these kinds of projects by the end of GD1, but usually begin working in these kinds of ways at the beginning of GD2. Some students are prop masters who make the 2D/3D assets, others learn to program for the Oculus, and others work to figure out the logic structures to make the puzzles work.

(Sean)HoloLens Experiences:

When we got into doing mixed reality development we weren't sure quite where we were headed or how to do it, because we were starting at the same time actual developers were starting but without the experience. This is where the rubber really meets the road in building the future. There aren't answers for how to do these kinds of projects right, and that is where we are always trying to get to.

1. HoloLight

   Students decided to create a game to teach people about light by making a game that would create a virtual LASER that would shoot out of a virtual emitter mounted to the ceiling in the room. Players would be able to place virtual mirrors in the room on various surfaces and change the orientation of the mirrors to create a way to bounce the virtual light around real objects to get it to an end point; this would require the use of the spatial mapping features of the HoloLens to create a map of the environment that would be overlaid on the real objects in the space. Students have created all of the coding that will create the mirrors, the light, the end point, and that controls the behavior of the light as it interacts with the different elements. We are hoping to release something to the Windows Store by the end of June 2018.

2. Courtyard Experience

The students and I realized that we could also create a less gamified version of software for the HoloLens, and so students began working on a courtyard experience that would allow a user to walk into our school courtyard where there are a variety of memorials and markers, and that user would be able to see virtual content that explained more about those memorials than just the information on them. We are currently hoping to create a virtual assistant, an information panel for each memorial, and voice/sound effects that would bring the memorial to life. There are technical aspects we are still working out, but are hoping to have something to showcase soon.

(Sean)Creating Arcade Cabinets:

Students are currently working on creating arcade cabinets that include buttons, joysticks, LED lighting, and other input methods populated with games created by my students to put in the school library. The goal is to move from productions that people don't often get to see into the production of experiences that expand out into the community. Students are planning, programming, engineering, and assembling these experiences from the ground up using resources the same way an independent game development studio would.

(Sean)Typical Class Activities:

Weeks 1-5:
We do tutorial work where students work with videos and with online tutorials that are pretty scripted to get the baseline skills they need to move on into tougher projects. For Unity these include the Roll-a-Ball tutorial, the Space Shooter tutorial, and the Survival Shooter tutorial. For students that go faster and quickly complete these tutorials, voluntary extensions are added, such as making new levels, adding new hazards, creating more significant win/loss conditions, and

adding in student identified expansions. For students that need to go slower, the kids all working with the videos and at their own pace frees me up to go around and help kids who are struggling.

Weeks 6-18:
We take a little time to identify the kinds of projects kids are interested in. Then, students are broken into groups based on their expressed interest in both the type of project to be done and their interest in the kind of role they want to play. We have artists, programmers, and team leads. Everyone works together on level design and project specs, and then when they have determined roles, they begin to work on pitching their idea for the project to me. Once projects are approved, the team lead…well, takes the lead on the team.

Daily:
I try to start the class with checking in with my team leads to see where they and their teams are at in the development process for their projects. We are working to have students use a Kanban approach to project management where I can monitor their efforts. To do this we use an online *post-it note* program. Students or team leads identify tasks, though sometimes I identify their tasks, and then team leads and students move tasks through the process of development. We use the categories: To Do – In Process – Needs Checking – Done. Only the teacher can move something from the *Needs Checking* to the *Done* column. We use Linoit.com as our post it site, because this site is free and will allow students to include documents, videos, audio clips, pictures, and is super easy to use. Any online program with the same functionality would work though.

(Sean)IB Comp Sci and Java Programming:

These classes are far more specific in the content taught and the process and methodologies of the course. Students are given more direct instruction and tutorials are far more aligned specifically to the IB curriculum, standards, and scope. We have, in the past, tried to teach the IB Computer Science course in one year, but this has been very difficult to do effectively because it is meant to be a two year course and the curriculum from the IB program is packed with Computer Science principles. The requirement is that students take on an independent assessment or IA in which they are supposed to identify a client with a real issue that can be solved with programming, go through the steps to interview that client, create a plan to address the client's need, create the development for that need according to the plan, create the software, do user testing, and then reflect on the process and meet with the client to get the client's reflection on the software and where they would like to see it go next.

In our typical schedule, students with no prior programming experience were supposed to take on that task and create the software for the client after less than four months of one hour a day programming classes. It was a very heavy lift, and we are currently looking to create a better model for how to approach these classes. Until we do, these courses are on hiatus.

(Sean) "On Grading":

It is difficult when working with the kinds of projects we are working on to always know what the end point will be. When we think we have it figured out, we often discover more problems to solve. Students are graded more on their ability to solve problems, work on teams, document evidence of their learning, project management, and contributions to both ideas and realizations of those ideas than on discrete coding or modelling skills. It would be easy to take the beaten path and simply give the kids tasks I know the answer to. It would be easy to give them tutorials and discrete skill quizzes that would verify their ability to extrude a model or successfully complete a loop; it is a different animal trying to inspire them to believe that they can go beyond and make something new. We have lots of discussions about their projects, and I spend a lot of time trying to figure out how to help them find the right resources to answer their questions. Many times it works, but sometimes it doesn't. Grading ebbs and flows as students have different needs and go at different paces, but all are engaged in learning how to be parts of teams and how to create knowledge with and for others – so that is where most of the grading in the class comes from.

(Sean)What Comes Next:

We try to build the future in classrooms of today. That means that we tackle big problems without predefined solutions. Students are trying to learn the software we use at the same time we are trying to use it for real purposes. We don't always know the answers and students spend a lot of time engaged in independent research to make their dreams of the future realities. We iterate...a lot. We start over and begin anew. We pick ourselves up and try to document all the ways we have discovered not to do things. Sometimes it leads to amazing work...and sometimes it leads to kids seeing the world in ways they never thought they would.

Final Thoughts

I hope I've challenged you to think out-of-the-box as you implement your own CS program. Or if you already have a solid program in place, I hope you have started to see the value of bringing in some big collaborative open-ended projects. Computer Science has found its way from an *extra elective class for a few* to a *required core class for many.* As you go down this road, my main point of advice is this:

There is an awesome energy and excitement around creating things using Computer Science tools. Make sure your classroom reflects that dynamic interaction and energy. Let exploration, students working together and figuring things out be a regular part of the CS experience. Don't fall into the trap of thinking that the only way a student can obtain information, knowledge, theory, and understanding is by being *told.* Your students are capable of being an active part of their own learning.

Immerse your students. Let them see it, feel it, engage with it, create something with it, struggle with it, and learn to love it. Find hands-on experiences that bring together their imagination, your passion, their passion, and their learning. Students don't mind hard work if they connect with it."

-Doug Bergman

Author Biography

Doug Bergman is Head of Computer Science at Porter-Gaud independent school in Charleston, SC. He has been the head of the CS department for 17+ years and been in CS education for 23+ years. For several years, he worked in industry as a programmer as well as in I.T. While attending and teaching school in the US, Japan, and France, he has traveled extensively across the globe. He is a product of public education K-16 and holds a Bachelor of Science in Computer Information Systems from Clemson University, M.A. in Education Administration from University of South Carolina, and is completing his Online Masters in Computer Science at Georgia Tech. He has taught in public schools, private schools, and professional schools and has worked with students from ages five to ninety-nine. His largest class was 300 students (I found out it was three hundred, not thirty, in the hallway on the way to class. That was fun.) He has experience developing his own curriculum as well as using existing curriculum developed by others. In addition to being honored with regional, state, national and international recognitions, he has presented at conferences worldwide. He has been an active member of the Microsoft Innovative Expert Educator program since 2011. In 2017, he was selected as a finalist for the Presidential Award for Excellence in Mathematics and Science Teaching. Currently, he serves on of the board of CSTA.